Location of the HETCH HETCHY quadrangle

Hetch Hetchy Reservoir

Thomas Winnett

High Sierra
Hiking Guide #12

HETCH HETCHY

by Ron Felzer

with the editors of
WILDERNESS PRESS
Thomas Winnett
editor-in-chief

Photos by the author
Except as noted

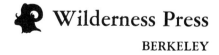 Wilderness Press

BERKELEY

ACKNOWLEDGMENTS

This second edition would be incomplete without acknowledgment of the immense amount of help I got from a number of Yosemite friends. I should like to thank in particular Grant Bunch for his assistance in the field; Dick Riegelhuth and Ron Mackie of the National Park Service for answering my many questions; Jeff Schaffer for his fantastic map and incredible amount of information about the park; Rich Reitnaver of the Yosemite Natural History Association; Tom Winnett, my best editor ever; and Wilma, whom I love lots.

— Ron Felzer
Berkeley, California
December, 1982

Dedicated to Ferdinand, guardian of Tioga Pass

First Edition 1973
Revised Second Printing 1981
SECOND EDITION 1983

Copyright © 1973, 1981, 1983 by Ron Felzer
Design by Thomas Winnett
Library of Congress Card Catalog No. 83-60455
International Standard Book No. 0-89997-030-3
Printed in the United States
Published by Wilderness Press
2440 Bancroft Way
Berkeley, CA 94704

Table of Contents

Introduction

THE HIGH SIERRA HIKING GUIDES from Wilderness Press are the first *complete* guides to the famous High Sierra. Each guide covers one 15-minute U.S.G.S. topographic quadrangle, which is an area about 14 miles east-west by 17 miles north-south. The inside front cover shows the location of the quadrangle covered by this guide.

There is a great and increasing demand for literature about America's favorite wilderness, John Muir's "Range of Light." To meet this demand, we have undertaken this guide series. The purpose of each book in the series is threefold: first, to provide a reliable basis for planning a trip; second, to serve as a field guide while you are on the trail; and third, to stimulate you to further field investigation and background reading. In each guide, there are a minimum of 100 described miles of trails, and the descriptions are supplemented with maps and other logistical and background information. HIGH SIERRA HIKING GUIDES are based on first-hand observation. There is absolutely no substitute for walking the trails, so we walked all the trails.

In planning this series, we chose the 15-minute quadrangle as the unit because—though every way of dividing the Sierra is arbitrary—the topographic quadrangle map ("topo map") is the chosen aid of almost every wilderness traveler. Inside the back cover of this book is an updated map of the quadrangle, showing the described trails. With this map, you can always get where you want to go, with a minimum of detours or wasted effort.

One other thing the wilderness traveler will need: a wilderness permit for all *overnight* stays in the Yosemite back-country. These required permits can be obtained in person during the summer and fall hiking seasons at the Yosemite Valley Visitor Center, the Big Oak Flat Entrance Information Center, the Tuolumne Meadows Wilderness Permit Kiosk and the Wawona Ranger Station. Generally from February 1 to May 31, wilderness permits may also be applied for by mail at:

Wilderness Permits
Box 577
Yosemite National Park, California 95389

The maximum group size permitted is 25 for hiking on maintained trails and 8 for cross-country travel. All back-country areas have visitor-use quotas, so it is best to apply early in the season and early in the day to be assured of getting onto the trail you want on the day you want. This is especially true for groups going into the Yosemite wilderness. These quotas are designed to minimize human impact on Yosemite's fragile environment while maximizing your enjoyment of it, so be sure to abide by the permit rules instituted by the Park Service to keep Yosemite natural and beautiful.

> "I don't know how people deal with their moods when they have no garden, raspberry patch or field to work in. You can take your angers, frustrations, bewilderments to the earth, working savagely, working up a sweat and an ache and a great weariness. The work rinses out the cup of your spirit, leaves it washed and clean and ready to be freshly filled with new hope.
>
> It is one of the reasons I am addicted to raspberry patches. The pie is purely symbolic."   Rachel Peden

The Country

THE YOSEMITE COUNTRY has been awing people for thousands of years. Its sky-piercing peaks and unbelievably deep canyons thrill today's visitors just as they have thrilled people since the first migrants from Asia gazed upon this land.

That part of Yosemite National Park described in this book is the northwest-central area of the park. This region includes the northern rim of Yosemite Valley, much of the Tioga Road corridor, the Grand Canyon of the Tuolumne River, Hetch Hetchy Reservoir, and some little-known but high-class wilderness to the north.

The highest elevation in *Hetch Hetchy* quadrangle, Mt. Hoffmann (10,850′), is several thousand feet shy of Mt. Lyell, the loftiest peak in the Park, located about 15 miles southeast. However, the walls of the Grand Canyon of the Tuolumne River in some places plunge more than 5000 feet in a horizontal distance of about 2 miles and so exceed Yosemite Valley's maximum depth by several hundred feet. The lack of spectacular summits in the Hetch Hetchy country is amply offset by the dramatic relief of its canyons.

Most of the country consists of rather low-profile, wooded ridges separated by deep, glacier-carved canyons. The average elevation of this quadrangle is about 7000 feet, which means summer comes sooner and winter comes later than in the higher parts of the Park. Hence hiking, especially near Hetch Hetchy Reservoir (elev. 3796′), can start earlier in the spring and continue later into the fall than it can in areas of the Park to the east and north. In fact, some of the trails in this guide are recommended only for early- or late-season travel because of midsummer heat.

Travelers seeking solitude here will not be disappointed, especially on the trails north of the Tuolumne River. They are only lightly used compared to routes nearer the Tioga Road and the Yosemite Valley rim, and they offer superb quietude.

Author at Pleasant Valley

However, true wilderness experiences await those hiking even in the more heavily traveled areas if they stick to the steeper and less direct routes between the trailheads and points of interest. Cross-country travel in the trailless regions near Mt. Hoffmann and along the South Fork Tuolumne River will bring peaceful rewards to the adventurous and *experienced* off-trail backpacker.

Students of landforms, wildlife and plants will find a great variety for their scrutiny in *Hetch Hetchy* quadrangle. As we noted, the Grand Canyon of the Tuolumne River is deeper than Yosemite Valley. Bird life characteristic of habitats from foothills to high summits can be seen here, and the plant spectrum ranges from Digger-pine woodlands to alpine fell fields.

Seekers of off-season back-country recreation in a landscape that presents some subtle contrasts to that of the High Sierra can find what they want here in *Hetch Hetchy*.

The History

EVEN A CURSORY LOOK at Hetch Hetchy quadrangle will reveal two prominent man-made features in this part of Yosemite National Park that have greatly influenced the character of this country and still do. These are Hetch Hetchy Reservoir and the Tioga Road.

The story of Hetch Hetchy is long and complicated, as is that of the Tioga Road. Both, of course, are intimately tied in with the history of Yosemite Valley and the Park as a whole, a tale which has been told many times elsewhere (see Recommended Readings at the end of the book). Here we will briefly outline the development of the Tioga Road as one of the main arteries into Yosemite National Park and across the Sierra Nevada before going into the story of Hetch Hetchy Reservoir in more detail.

The Great Sierra Wagon Road was completed in 1883 for the purpose of hauling ore from the Tioga Mine, just east of Tioga Pass, to the western foothills. The mine failed in 1884, with apparently no ore ever having been shipped out on the road. For the next 31 years ownership of the road changed hands several times, and more than once a bill to authorize its purchase by the Federal government was defeated in Congress. It was finally bought by several private individuals (including future first Director of the National Park Service, Stephen T. Mather) and groups such as the Modesto Chamber of Commerce, and title to the road was given to the U.S. on April 10, 1915.

The road was opened officially to the public that year, and by 1916 nearly 600 cars had entered the Park from the east. The road gained in popularity through the 1920s, but there were many complaints about its roughness and dust. As early as 1925, plans were being laid to rebuild or relocate portions of the road for safer driving and easier maintenance. By July of 1938 the lower and upper ends of the road had been rebuilt and the central part from McSwain Meadow to Cathedral Creek had been oiled. No more dust! It was not till 1961, however, that the Tioga Road's present 46-mile route from Crane Flat to Tioga Pass was finished.

Today the Tioga Road cuts across the middle of Yosemite National Park, giving access to the heart of *Hetch Hetchy* quadrangle. How ironic that the original road to a failing mine would probably never have been built had its promoters realized that they would never be able to use it. This area would probably still be wilderness today, for only six years after the Tioga Mine was closed Yosemite became a national park.

Hetch Hetchy Valley once rivaled Yosemite Valley itself in grandeur and in rugged beauty. It was a deep, flat-bottomed valley of lush meadows, with glorious stands of oak and pine. The Ahwahnechee and Paiute Indians came yearly to gather acorns and to grind them in bedrock mortars. Two waterfalls—Tueeulala in spring and Wapama all year long—plunged off its northern cliffs into the Tuolumne River, which meandered languidly below. The valley's name comes from the Indian word "atch atchie," for a grain mix made with a variety of grass and other edible seeds. Today Hetch Hetchy Valley lies drowned under 400 feet of water.

It was either Nate or Joe Screech—it depends on the account—who was the first white man to see Hetch Hetchy. On a hunting trip in the late 1840s one of these brothers saw the valley but was unable to get down to the floor. He later asked an old chief, who claimed the land in that area, about this valley. The chief replied that there was no valley, but that if Screech did find one, it would be his.

A few years later, in 1850, Nate Screech, probably in the company of his brothers Joe and Bill, found his way into the valley and discovered the very same chief there with his wives. A little surprised, but keeping his promise, the chief had the women pack up, telling them they had to leave as he had promised Screech the valley and must keep his word. Such were the beginnings of the end for Hetch Hetchy Valley.

7

Hetch Hetchy Valley before the dam

Joe Screech built the first trail into the valley, from Big Oak Flat 38 miles away, and for many years the valley was used by sheepmen and cattlemen, as well as by Paiutes for acorn gathering.

John Muir first entered Hetch Hetchy Valley in 1870. He had this to say about what he saw:

> Hetch Hetchy Valley is a grand landscape garden, one of nature's rarest and most precious mountain mansions. As in Yosemite, the sublime rocks of its walls glow with life, whether leaning back in repose or standing erect in thoughtful attitudes giving welcome to the storms and calms alike.

Thirty-one years later, San Francisco Mayor James O. Phelan made the first filing with the Department of the Interior for the use of Hetch Hetchy as a reservoir for the municipal water supply of the city. This request was turned down by then Secretary of the Interior Hitchcock. The Sierra Club, and particularly its president John Muir, worked unceasingly to prevent the desecration of this "mountain mansion." However, San Francisco's continuing application for the damming of Hetch Hetchy bore fruit in 1908, when Secretary Garfield granted the city the right to use the valley as a reservoir. But the battle for Hetch Hetchy was to rage for five more years.

President William Howard Taft visited Yosemite in 1909, and Muir was able to convince him of the necessity of preserving the pristine beauty of Hetch Hetchy from exploitation as a reservoir site. Taft's Interior Secretary, Richard Ballinger, opposed the dam builders throughout the remainder of Taft's term of office.

From 1910 through 1913 a series of hearings were held to examine the city's need for Hetch Hetchy as a water reservoir when there were other possible sources, such as a Calaveras dam. Finally, Congressman John E. Raker, with the aid of Senator Key Pittman of Nevada, steered a bill through Congress—the Raker Act—authorizing the use of Hetch Hetchy and Eleanor Creek as municipal water sources for the City of San

Francisco. This bill was signed by President Woodrow Wilson on December 19, 1913. The city had won, and the preservationists had lost.

Or had they? Muir thought "some compensating good must follow." Indeed, the creation of the National Park Service in 1916 with a strong edict "to preserve the natural and historic objects" in the parks can be seen as a very positive response to this greatest invasion of the National Parks and the National Park idea that the American people yet have allowed. In recent years this 1916 law has been instrumental in defeating proposals for damming the Grand Canyon and inundating Park-system lands in Grand Canyon National Monument, as well as affecting the ancient flow of the Colorado River through Grand Canyon National Park. The conservation forces were united by the Hetch Hetchy battle, and the conservation movement continued to grow despite this defeat.

What of the dam itself? Construction of O'Shaughnessy Dam—named for Chief Engineer M. M. O'Shaughnessy—started in 1919 and was completed in May 1923. Some 390,000 cubic yards of concrete were poured, and over six million board feet of lumber were cut—within the Park!—in completing the dam. Water from the reservoir first started flowing into San Francisco in 1934. The dam's height was raised an additional 86 feet in 1938, producing a final reservoir area of 1972 acres with a volume of over 117 billion gallons.

Today Hetch Hetchy Reservoir exists almost solely as a source of water and power for the City of San Francisco, and there is really little of value here for the rest of the American people (fishing from the shore is permitted). Would it be too presumptuous to ask that our legislators consider the restoration of Hetch Hetchy Valley to its natural state after the dam has been made obsolete by better utilization and conservation of water from Lake Eleanor, Cherry Lake and local sources? A "modest proposal," no doubt. But think of its benefits: improving the land, setting back the clock to a more pristine time, increasing the number of beautiful places on the earth for a change, instead of decreasing them. Think of the jobs it would create: tearing down the dam, hauling the concrete away, removing the silt, restoring the valley, its trees, meadows and wildlife. Should we not be optimists and consider the generations one, two, or even three hundred years from now, when surely Hetch Hetchy Valley will have recovered, in the words of Harriet Monroe, its own individuality:

> It was a garden of paradise, this Valley; a lesser Yosemite, but very different, with an infinitely charming individuality of its own; smaller but more compact, less grand but no less beautiful. In its wonderful forest growth of great variety and magnificent development it surpasses that of Yosemite Valley itself.

Glacial erratic on Tenaya-Tuolumne Trail

The Geology

THE STORY THE ROCKS tell is one of change: a tale of uplift and erosion; of seas invading and receding; of glaciers advancing and receding. The only constant is the rate: slow. Slow by our standards, for we have seen the world with human eyes for mere seconds of the earth's time.

Over 400 million years ago the present area of the Sierra Nevada was covered by a shallow sea. The sediments that piled up on the bottom of this sea became rocks of sandstone, shale and limestone which were gradually uplifted and thrust into a range of mountains. The sea retreated. But the rains fell and the rivers eroded. These mountains were reduced; and the sea returned. The sediments reaccumulated.

Starting about 200 million years ago, during the time of the dinosaurs, these new sediments were folded and pushed up by molten granitic rock from below. This intruding granite would become the backbone of the Sierra we know today. Erosion continued while mammals evolved upon the earth after dinosaurs died out.

As these secondary mountains were carried away by water and gravity, filling what was to become the Central Valley, the granite core of the Sierra was further uplifted, sloping toward the west. A few million years ago the eastern part of this pre-Sierra mass began slipping downward along faults, forming the Mono Basin, the Owens Valley and other down-faulted *grabens,* and leaving a very high and steep scarp, or fault-face, on the east side of the range. This movement continues today.

The valleys and ridges of the Sierra were then subjected to a final carving and polishing that produced the landscape we see today. Numerous times in the last 3 million years or so, rivers of ice called glaciers flowed down from the peaks, when more snow was falling in winter than was melting in summer. These rivers of ice advanced down the valleys and even over the ridges, leaving their marks throughout the high country and down as low as 4000 feet in elevation. The prime examples of glacial sculpting in Hetch Hetchy quadrangle are the Grand Canyon of the Tuolumne River and its tributary canyons.

Scratches in the exposed bedrock, called striations, and polish on the bedrock surface are the work of rocky debris carried in the bottoms of glaciers, so they tell us where glaciers were and which way they moved. Lake Vernon has fine examples around it.

Hanging valleys such as the valleys of Ten Lakes Creek and Cathedral Creek high above the Tuolumne canyon show how much faster the Tuolumne glacier cut down than did its much smaller tributary glaciers.

Piles of debris called moraines left at the sides and the snout of wasted glaciers exist throughout this land, as at Harden Lake and above Snow Creek near the Tioga Road.

The moving ice, with its rock grinders, also left characteristically shaped *roches moutonnées* on the floors of the valleys they scraped over. These outcrops of bedrock granite having gently sloping, smooth upstream sides and steep, rough downstream faces are found easily in the Grand Canyon of the Tuolumne itself.

Today the glaciers are gone from *Hetch Hetchy,* and only the briefest of remnants cling to the northeast walls of the high peaks to the east. They may come again, as may the seas, as will the rain and the wind, and the Sierra will continue to change.

The Climate

CALIFORNIA'S WEATHER, and hence that of the Sierra Nevada, is governed by what goes on thousands of miles away, out over the Pacific Ocean. There, a permanent system of high pressure called the Pacific High moves north and south with the yearly march of the sun. In summer it is west of central California; in winter it lies off the Baja California coast.

When the Pacific High sits between the California coast and the subpolar low-pressure cell in the Gulf of Alaska during summer, it tends to keep the North Pacific's storms, bred in this low, from reaching the state. However, during the winter, when the Pacific High is farther south, and also is not as strong, the subpolar low has increased in intensity. That's when storms move off the ocean and over the land, and California gets rained or snowed on. Actually, it's not all that simple, but this brief sketch does help explain why about 50% of precipitation in *Hetch Hetchy* occurs in the winter, while only 5% or so comes during the summer, when most readers of this guide are likely to visit the mountains.

What about that 5%? It usually takes the form of short, summer-afternoon thunderstorms. When hot air from the Central Valley rises up the slopes of the Sierra, it cools at a rate of about 5.5°F per 1000 feet of altitude gain. In addition, the air over heat-radiating surfaces in the high country, such as an expanse of whitish granite, may also rise convectionally. When air rises, for whatever reason, it cools, and may drop its moisture. A thundershower is born. It "never rains in the Sierra in summer"—but raingear and a small tent are not that heavy, and wet sleeping bags aren't much fun.

Summer temperatures in the mountains vary with elevation and *aspect*—compass orientation. Generally, the temperature in *stable* air decreases by about 3.6°F for every 1000-foot gain in elevation. So, disregarding aspect, a difference in temperature of 25°F can be expected between Hetch Hetchy Reservoir—the lowest point in the quad—and Mt. Hoffmann—the highest—due to the change in elevation alone. No one is likely to make this trip in one day, but the possibilities are dramatic. When we add to this the evaporative and convective effects of wind, a windless 75° afternoon at Hetch Hetchy turns into a chilling experience on bare skin of 30° at the summit of Mt. Hoffmann, assuming a 25-mile-per-hour wind there. A windbreaker is another vital piece of summer paraphernalia.

One last comment on climate: solar radiation reaching the earth's surface increases with elevation. There is up to four times as much ultraviolet at high elevations as at sea level, and ultraviolet energy causes sunburn and can lead to skin cancer. So visitors to the high country who burn easily, or who haven't acquired at least a good tan by the time they start living out in the sun, do well to liberally apply a good ultraviolet screen while here, or to otherwise cover their skin from the damaging rays of the sun during the heat of the day.

Snow Plant

The Flora

OTHER GUIDES IN THIS
series have described the more
colorful wildflowers and the
dominant trees of the high country. *Hetch Hetchy* quadrangle,
however, includes some low-elevation plant associations of the
western Sierran slope not found in most other High Sierra
quadrangles. So in this guide we will discuss some of the trees
living near the lower limits of winter snow—around 3000–6000
feet elevation.

Black Oak

One of the most conspicuous and important of the broadleaf trees in the lower forest zone of Yosemite National Park
is California black oak (*Quercus kelloggii*). This is a deciduous
tree found at about 4000–6000 feet in this part of the Sierra.
From a distance the tree has a broad, rounded crown, totally
unlike the conifers with which it associates.

A closer look reveals large (to 10″ x 6″) green, deeply lobed
leaves with sharp spines at the tips of the lobes. The bark on
older trees is black and checkered. The acorns about one inch
long that mature in the fall are an important food in the diets
of mule deer, tree squirrels, ground squirrels, and band-tailed
pigeons and other birds. Up until the early years of this century, the Yosemite Indians used these same fruits as a major
item in their diet. Bedrock mortars where black-oak acorns
were ground into meal are found many places in Yosemite—in
this quadrangle at Tiltill Valley, for example.

Golden Oak

Another common broadleaf tree at lower elevations on the
western slope is the golden oak (*Quercus chrysolepis*). Golden
oak, also called goldencup, canyon, white and maul oak, is an
evergreen, or live, oak tree. It keeps its small, leathery, irregu-
larly toothed leaves for several years before they fall off. Its
name comes from the appearance of the acorns in late summer

and early autumn. The nut, about one inch long, is partly en-
closed in a cap covered with dense, woolly, yellow fuzz. The
underside of this tree's leaves characteristically have a thin
dusting of this golden fuzz. Golden oak is the second-largest
of California oaks (after valley oak) and its dense, straight-
grained wood has long been used in tool handles and in construction. Its acorns are also a staple in the diets of numerous
birds, mammals and insects. Golden oak is common around
Hetch Hetchy Reservoir and on the Yosemite Creek trail below
Yosemite Falls.

California Bay

California bay (*Umbellularia californica*), or laurel, is known
to most people who do much cooking. The leaves of this tree
contain aromatic substances that have long made it valuable
not only as a spice but also in folk medicine. Cinnamon, cam-
phor, sassafras and other essences come from related trees
found largely in tropical forests. California's laurel, or bay, has
evergreen elliptical leaves about 4 inches long and an olive-like
fruit whose pit is edible when dried. Bay can tolerate deep
shade, and throughout much of its range it is a late successional
species, tending to thrive even in the shade of the great coastal
redwoods. Theoretically it could eventually replace these trees
should natural fire and flood—to which redwood is better
adapted—be prevented by human activities. In *Hetch Hetchy*
quadrangle we find bay trees near Mirror Lake, around Hetch
Hetchy Reservoir, and on the Yosemite Creek trail at elevations generally below 6000 feet.

Digger Pine

Among the coniferous, or cone-bearing, trees of the Sierra,
several barely get above the foothills. Digger pine (*Pinus
sabiniana*) is one of these. It is found in the Coast Ranges of
California and on the western slope of the central Sierra to an
elevation of about 4000 feet. Its name is a derogatory one

based on the contemptuous terms applied to the Indians who used this tree's large seeds and green cones for food. The 49'ers and others called the Indians "Diggers" and so too the tree. The Digger pine looks rather scrawny, with sparse, smoke-blue foliage and reddish, plated bark. The cones are large, with hooks on the ends of the scales. The needles are up to 12 inches long, grouped in clumps of three. Digger pine is common in this quadrangle only around Hetch Hetchy Reservoir.

Douglas-Fir

Another of the many coniferous trees of the Sierra is Douglas-fir (*Pseudotsuga menziesii*), occurring in the west-central portion of the range at elevations from 2000 to 7000 feet. Unlike Digger pine, Douglas-fir typically exhibits the "excurrent" growth form of cone-bearing trees—that is, one main trunk with a number of whorls of horizontal limbs branching from it. Douglas-fir, which ranges from British Columbia to northern Mexico, is the single most important lumber tree in the United States. In *Hetch Hetchy* quadrangle it does not grow to great size except near Tenaya Creek just above Mirror Lake. The species is known by its 3-inch-long cones and their *exserted* bracts—papery structures that stick *out* of a cone above each scale. Its needles are flat and single, not bundled as in the pines. Finally, Douglas-fir can be told from red and white fir—which it resembles superficially—by its buds, which are *always* pointed. Red- and white-fir buds are blunt-tipped. Ecologically, Douglas-fir thrives where occasional fires keep the forest open and allow its light-requiring seedlings to grow. Little new growth of Douglas-fir is seen under old, dense, shady stands, because other trees, such as incense-cedar (see below) and the true firs, are much better adapted to these conditions.

Incense-Cedar

Incense-cedar (*Calocedrus decurrens*) has the widest range in Yosemite National Park of any of the trees we are discussing. It grows on the western slope of the central Sierra between 2000 and 7000 feet. This tree is not a *true* cedar—hence the hyphen in its common name—but a member of the cypress family. The true cedars (like the cedars of Lebanon) are in the pine family! That's plant classification for you. Incense-cedars supply the wood for pencils, so the next time you sharpen a pencil, smell the shavings and catch the odor of incense-cedar wood. The leaves of this tree are quite different from the leaves of the previous two species. They are like reptile scales, overlapping on the branchlets, and are usually less than ½ inch long. The cone is distinctive, being less than 1½ inches long and having only six scales. Two of these enlarge and open partway to give the cone the appearance of a duck's bill. Incense-cedar grows well under the shade of other species, such as ponderosa pine, Jeffrey pine and Douglas-fir, and it becomes the dominant species in a stand where fires have not occurred for many decades.

Many other kinds of trees, as well as shrubs, wildflowers and ferns, are mentioned in the trail descriptions of this guidebook. The reader who wants further enlightenment about the flora of *Hetch Hetchy* may acquire one or more of the excellent references dealing with this subject that are listed at the end of this book.

The Fauna

IT IS BEYOND THE SCOPE OF this trail guide to discuss all the hundreds of birds, mammals, reptiles and other higher animals found in the *Hetch Hetchy* quadrangle, and it is probably not even possible to describe all the thousands of insects, roundworms and other lesser forms that live here. In this volume of the High Sierra Hiking Guide series, then, we will describe just three of what may be termed more *problematical* kinds of animals that wilderness travellers may encounter in the *Hetch Hetchy* Yosemite.

Undoubtedly the most bothersome of the animal life found in *Hetch Hetchy* quadrangle—and in most of the High Sierra—is the ubiquitous mosquito. Three types occur in the Sierra, at different elevations. *Anopheles* inhabits the Central Valley and the foothills of the Sierra. This type—or genus—is the main carrier of malaria in places where the malarial parasite is found. Today there is no known malaria in California mosquito populations, but people carrying the parasite could infect local mosquito populations. *Anopheles* adults lay their eggs in pools and ponds, where the eggs float individually. The larvae, or "wrigglers," of all species of mosquito must come to the surface for air. *Anopheles* larvae lie parallel to the water surface when breathing. Adult *Anopheles* females, which require a meal of blood to complete egg production (as do the other females), can be told from the others by the *tilted* position of their bodies while they are sucking blood from a host. *Anopheles* are not likely to be much of a problem in the foothills after May or June, when most winter runoff ponds have dried up.

Culex, which can carry encephalitis virus, is found up into the yellow-pine belt, where their eggs are laid in still pools of water. *Culex* eggs float together in a mass on the surface of the water, and each larva is equipped with a siphonlike breathing tube which allows it to breathe surface air while hanging down vertically in the water. The female in feeding position

holds her body nearly *horizontal. Culex* will give campers a
hard time from the last cold weather in spring until July.

Aedes mosquitoes are found worldwide from the tropics to
the Arctic tundra. The only terrestrial area they haven't been
found in is Antarctica. In much of the world *Aedes* are carriers
of disease; in particular they are carriers of several types of
yellow-fever virus, which is *not* found in California. In the
Sierra, *Aedes* occurs from the foothills to elevations over
10,000 feet. This genus is the one campers are most likely to
notice at subalpine lakes in late July or early August. Usually
after mid-August it is hard to find a mosquito in the Sierra.
Aedes will breed any place there is standing water: snowmelt
puddles, marshes, holes in stumps, etc. The eggs can sit high
and dry for several months, then hatch after a rain or snowmelt.

One protection from mosquitoes is to avoid the mountains
when they are most abundant. Their numbers peak in late May
at about 4000 feet, and advance upward as the snow melts,
peaking at 10,000 feet around late July. However, unfortunately, these are also the months when the mountains are
most beautiful: wildflowers are at their peak, the days are long,
water is plentiful, storms are rare, and late snow patches offer
many delights—from snowballs to snow cones or a background
for photogenic scenes. What to do? Cover the skin, especially
in early evening, when mosquitoes are usually the most active.
It is good to have long pants and a long-sleeved shirt, as well
as some kind of hat. Tents with mosquito-net screens are in-
valuable. Some people, in fact, require head nets when the
bugs are particularly hungry. Of course, these days we use
chemicals for everything, and there are some effective mosquito repellents. Repellents containing the active ingredient
N, N-diethyl-meta-toluamide have been proved best. Nothing
else commonly available is nearly so effective. Taking vitamin-
B_1 pills and not eating bananas have been suggested, but they
have yet to be proved as generally effective methods. Of
course, air temperature, wind, vegetation, location of standing

water, the previous winter's snow, last year's mosquito season, individual body chemistry and a person's own outdoor experience all influence whether one will be bugged by mosquitoes. Much research needs to be done on this piercing subject.

A somewhat larger, more feared, and much more misunderstood member of the *Hetch Hetchy* fauna is the rattlesnake. The kind found here is the northern Pacific rattlesnake, a variety of the western rattlesnake (*Crotalus viridis*).

All poisonous snakes in North America north of Mexico (except for the coral snake) are in the pit-viper subfamily. Our western rattlesnake, the only poisonous snake in California, is one of them. This means they have loreal pits, or heat-sensitive organs, on each side of the face between the eye and the nostril with which to detect warm-blooded prey. Other prey is probably detected by movement. The way rattlesnakes kill their prey is to strike with the mouth held wide open. Two hollow fangs are plunged into the prey, and as the jaw is pulled shut, venom sacs at the base of the fangs are squeezed, injecting venom into the victim. Unlike coral-snake venom, which is a nerve poison, rattlesnake venom affects the circulatory system.

In *Hetch Hetchy* quadrangle, rattlesnakes are common in the Grand Canyon of the Tuolumne River, especially near Pate Valley. They are active only during the warmer months, when they seek the sun except in hot middays. In hot weather, they may be active at night. Their brown color and diamond-shaped back patches blend in well with their background, especially dried leaves.

The rattlesnake fills a natural and vital niche in this mountain ecosystem. It is an efficient predator of ground squirrels, mice, rats and some birds and lizards, and thereby helps to keep populations of these animals from overrunning their food supply or getting into other problems caused by overpopulation. Rattlesnakes themselves—especially the younger ones—may be prey for some larger animals, such as hawks and owls.

Hikers are in little danger of dying from the bite of a rattlesnake. In fact, most hikers in *Hetch Hetchy* will never see one. However, when one is encountered, backpackers should be aware of what's happening. Usually the snake is going the other way. Humans are larger than rattlesnakes, so unless cornered, the snake will retreat—a law of the wild. If you meet a rattler coiled and rattling, ready to strike, leave it alone. Don't tease it—let it go its way. They rarely strike farther than 12 inches, and ankle-high boots are good protection should one surprise a snake behind a log or rock. When using your hands climbing in rattlesnake country, watch where you put them.

In case of rattlesnake bite, lay the patient down, keep him quiet and go for help.

Another member of the *Hetch Hetchy* fauna sure to be of interest, in conversation if not in the flesh, is the black bear (*Ursus americanus*). There are no longer any grizzly bears in California; the last killing of one occurred in 1922. The cinnamon-colored bruins seen today are merely color phases of the black bear.

There has been a profound change in attitude toward the black bear by the Park Service during the past 40 years. When Yosemite first became a popular recreation spot, tourists wanted to see bears as much as they do today. The difference between now and then was that these desires were catered to in a foolish fashion. The Park Service actually fed the bears regularly during the summer at feeding pits in Yosemite Valley. This practice soon led to problems.

Relieved of a natural control on their population—amount of food available—the number of bears mushroomed to about ten times the natural carrying capacity of the Valley. The animals lost their fear of humans, and they began raiding campers' food stocks and attacking people—as many as sixty cases reported in one season. Was this the purpose of a National Park? No—it had become a zoo! So Park policy changed in 1940 back to what it should have been—and that was, in this case, to preserve the naturalness of the fauna. So about 50 bears were removed from the Valley to remote parts of the Park, and it became illegal to feed, tease or molest any bears in the Park. Finally, in the early 1970s, 30 years later, the bear situation was approaching normality; the Park Service was even getting around to replacing its bear-ly adequate garbage cans with fairly bear-proof refuse containers in the campgrounds. One style of bear-proof container was even invented by park personnel.

Our concern here, however, is with the back-country bear, and not the garbage bear. So, to help these still wild animals and to help ourselves, how should we conduct ourselves when traveling in bear country?

Young black bear

The hiker's first concern should be the type of food carried and how it is stored. Generally, it's not wise to pack fresh meat or other odoriferous foods where bears are common in this area: Pate Valley, Rancheria Creek, Tiltill Valley and White Wolf especially. A pack or sack containing food should *never* be left unattended for more than a few minutes. Backpackers have been known to lose portions of their food rations in the time it takes to walk a few yards to a stream and back. At night or on day hikes away from camp, food should be suspended from a tree limb using the technique illustrated in the backcountry handout you received when you got your wilderness permit. If you are above timberline, you must either find a cliff bears can't climb or find a deep crack in a boulder where bears can't reach the bottom. Of course food in a crack is available to small animals, so if you see no signs of bears in the vicinity of your camp, you may want to guard against the small ones and hope for no bears, though this is tempting fate. Finally, cleaning cooking and eating utensils in the evening before bed reduces the attraction of one's campsite.

On the trail, most hikers who meet black bears see them going off at a gallop in the other direction. They usually fear people, but if a sow with cubs is seen, take every precaution not to get between her and her cubs and leave the area as judiciously as possible. Black bears rarely attack humans unless provoked, so courtesy here repays itself.

Occasionally, a bear that repeatedly raids tents and food larders is shot because it has become dangerous to humans. This is a sad occurrence for us and for the bear. So, to reiterate the signs, brochures and verbal pleas: *Park bears are wild; do not feed or bother them.*

For more detailed information on the animals of Yosemite National Park and the High Sierra, the reader's attention is called to the many valuable references listed at the end of this book, and to the information sheets available from the Park Service.

Mountain Manners

WHEN JOHN MUIR roamed through the Sierra during the last century, he made camp wherever he happened to be at day's end by cutting branches to sleep on and building a large bonfire to warm himself through the night. Muir was innocent, and there was virtually no one else wandering the mountains in those days. But can you imagine what the Yosemite backcountry would be like today if every backpacker did that? Because there are thousands of hikers out on Yosemite's wilderness trails these days, each of us must treat the fragile wilderness environment as if there were very little of it left (which is true), particularly when making camp.

Park Service rules reasonably require that you make camp only in previously established sites. No new fire rings should be made anywhere in the backcountry. We at Wilderness Press recommend that only stoves be used for cooking and that burning of wood for any reason be kept to a minimum. In Yosemite, no wood fires are allowed at all above 9600 feet elevation.

Campsites should be *at least 100 feet* from streams, lakes, and trails, where the terrain permits, and in any case should never be closer than 25 feet. Camp only in timbered or sandy areas, for they can take more abuse than fragile meadows. No live plants should be cut for any purpose, and the need for unsightly trenches around tent sites can be avoided by pitching camp in a well-drained area.

All litter and garbage which cannot be completely burned should be transported out of the wilderness the way it was brought in: in your pack. No debris of any kind should be left to mar the natural scenery, and this includes such natural but not easily degradable materials as orange peels and such unnatural materials as plastic bags, aluminum foil and baggie ties. No garbage should be buried, as it would be dug up and scattered by animals.

All dish and other washing—including tooth brushing—should be done *at least 100 feet* from lakes and streams, and the used water scattered in well-vegetated areas. No pollutants of any kind should enter streams or lakes, and this includes so-called "biodegradable" soaps and toothpastes.

Sierran waters are apparently becoming contaminated with parasites that can cause severe diarrhea and other intestinal problems. Implicated in several cases is the protozoan *Giardia lamblia,* which can be carried and spread by humans as well as by domestic and wild animals. Park rules require that, to prevent the spread of this and other potential disease organisms in our surface waters, all human waste disposal be *at least 150 feet* from any water source, as well as trails, camping areas and meadows. Feces should be buried in a hole 5 to 6 inches deep, and toilet paper should be carried out in plastic bags if it cannot be safely burned. It is recommended that all drinking water from untreated sources be boiled to avoid contracting intestinal parasites. Chemical treatments are not now considered reliable in killing all contaminating organisms.

Finally, a national park is for people to enjoy nature and its wildlife. It is not the place for barking, game-chasing dogs. Park Service rules prohibit pets on all trails. So leave yours at home; do not take it into the backcountry where it will annoy other hikers, harass wildlife, pollute campsites and possibly import diseases harmful to native animals.

The wildlands of North America, such as the Hetch Hetchy Yosemite, are among the very last *hospitable* places on earth that have not been completely abused by humanity, technological or otherwise. It's their last stand, and ours. As Thoreau so succinctly put it, "in wildness is the preservation of the world." It's up to us.

The Trails

ALL THE TRAILS DESCRIBED in this guidebook lie within the boundaries of Yosemite National Park. They are among the best-maintained and best-signed trails in the Sierra. The more heavily used trails, such as the one to Ten Lakes, receive yearly grooming, whereas less popular routes, such as the Smith Meadow trail, get maintenance at somewhat longer intervals. As of now, there is no policy in Yosemite to allow trails to revert to nature, as the Forest Service has begun to do in some of its parts of the Sierra. Using this guidebook and the updated *Hetch Hetchy* topographic map inside the back cover, one should have no problem finding one's route here.

The attractions of *Hetch Hetchy* quadrangle are accessible to hikers through a wide variety of trails. This book divides trails into three categories: day hikes, backpack trails and lateral trails.

Day Hikes. We have designated all the trails in *Hetch Hetchy* quadrangle south of the Tioga Road—as well as several to the north—as day-hike trails, because the average hiker in good condition can cover any of these in a few hours' to a day's walking. Most of the descriptions run downhill from the Tioga Road to Yosemite Valley. One exception is the Snow Creek (Tenaya Lake and Tuolumne Meadows) trail, which is described uphill from Yosemite Valley to the Tioga Road. Several of the day hikes are suitable as overnight backpack trails if your inclination is to spend more time on one. This is particularly true of the Yosemite Creek trail, which has many fine possible campsites along the stream. Be sure to check for restrictions when picking up your required wilderness permit from the Park Service.

Backpack Trails. Most of the trails north of the Tioga Road, except those to Harden Lake and to Lukens Lake and the short lateral trails, have been designated as backpack trails. These are overnight routes which require a minimum of two days' travel and one night—at least—of camping out. Some of the shorter backpack trails, such as the one to Lake Vernon via Beehive and the one to Ten Lakes, could be done in and out by expert hikers in one day, but that would definitely be pushing it. For several of the longer backpacks, like the one into Rodgers Lake, we recommend *at least* three days, except for ultramarathoners.

Lateral Trails. Four lateral trails are described in this guide. They connect day-hike or backpack trails to points of interest or give access from an alternate trailhead to a main trail.

THE TRAILHEADS

A trailhead is where a trail starts. Seven are described below. An additional trailhead, not included below, begins at Sunnyside Campground (the old Camp 4) in Yosemite Valley, from which hikers who wish to may do the Yosemite Creek trail or the North Dome trail in the reverse direction from the description in the guidebook.

Unfortunately, the city has come to the mountains in more ways than one, so here is a word of caution about parking at trailheads: do not leave valuables of any kind in a parked vehicle. Chances are good they won't be there when you get back, even if locked in the glove compartment or trunk. Money, credit cards and cameras are especially likely to be taken.

And don't leave food in sight or smell of bears. They will take it and leave you with a broken car.

Tioga Road at Yosemite Creek: The Ten Lakes and Yosemite Creek trails start about 100 yards west of the Yosemite Creek crossing of the Tioga Road (Highway 120). Park on either side of the road west of Yosemite Creek. Map section F3.

Tioga Road Intermediate: The trailheads for alternate and lateral routes to Lukens Lake and the Yosemite Creek trail, respectively, are on the Tioga Road about 3½ miles west of Yosemite Creek. Parking is ample. Map sections E3, 4.

Tamarack Creek: This trailhead is at a small parking area on the south side of the road 2½ miles east of the turnoff to Tamarack Flat Campground (Gin Flat) along the Tioga Road. Map section C5.

White Wolf: White Wolf resort and campground is about a mile north of the Tioga Road, 14 miles east of Crane Flat. Trails to Harden Lake, Lukens Lake, the Grand Canyon of the Tuolumne, Pleasant Valley, Rodgers Lake and Smith Meadow begin here across the road from the store. Map section E3.

Porcupine Creek: This trailhead for the North Dome trail is beside the Tioga Road just 1.1 miles east of the Porcupine Flat Campground turnoff and 2.1 miles west of the May Lake turnoff. Map section G4.

Hetch Hetchy Reservoir: Just 1.1 miles outside the Park's Big Oak Flat entrance station, leave Highway 120 and drive north 7.4 miles on Evergreen Road to its junction with the Hetch Hetchy Road. Turn right and go 9.1 miles to the large parking area at O'Shaughnessy Dam. Trails to Lake Vernon and to Pleasant Valley begin here. Map section B2.

Mirror Lake: In Yosemite Valley, take the upper valley shuttle bus to the Mirror Lake bus stop, about a mile below the former lake. Map section F6.

Trail Descriptions

(The map coordinates of the start of a trail appear at the end of the material that introduces the trail.)

The route descriptions that follow may mention *ducks, cairns* or *blazes*. A duck is one or several small rocks placed in such a way that the placement is obviously not natural. A cairn is a number of small rocks made into a pile. A blaze is usually a dotted i- (or more rarely a T-) shaped scar chopped into a tree's bark at about eye level.

The mileage for nearly all the trails is, as indicated in the descriptions, the one-way distance, not the round-trip distance. The net elevation change is also given and, where there are appreciable ups in a generally down trail or vice versa, the total elevation change is also given. Average hikers can use these figures to estimate how much time a hike will take them, allowing roughly one hour for each two miles of distance, and an additional hour for each 1000 feet of elevation gain or 2000 feet of elevation loss.

All map references are to the updated 1980 Wilderness Press edition of the *Hetch Hetchy* quadrangle which comes with this guidebook.

Shuttle trips require one of the following: a vehicle at each end of the hike, someone to drive a single vehicle from a trailhead around to trail's end, re-walking the trail in reverse, working out a loop trip, hitchhiking, or use of the free Valley shuttle bus or the daily round-trip motorcoach between Yosemite Valley and Lee Vining. Check with the Yosemite Park and Curry Company for current rates and schedules of this cross-Park bus.

Left: Yosemite Creek above Yosemite Falls

Day Hike #1   **Yosemite Creek Trail**

Tioga Road to Yosemite Valley

12 miles one way; net loss 3520$'$; total loss 4180$'$

Shuttle trip. F3.

A long day hike to Yosemite Valley for the experienced hiker, this trip can be made into an overnight trip by those who would like to spend more than one day enjoying the country along Yosemite Creek and its numerous emerald-green pools.

From the trailhead on the south side of the Tioga Road a few hundred feet west of Yosemite Creek, the trail parallels the road west for several hundred yards and then cuts south toward Yosemite Creek through a stand of lodgepole and Jeffrey pine, red fir and western juniper over a dense understory of huckleberry oak. We soon meet the creek in a stand of aspens and make an easy crossing on rocks or logs downstream.

The path continues south, parallel to and just above the stream, as we descend to Yosemite Creek Campground, which is on the Old Tioga Road. From here we follow the road southwest ½ mile through the campground and then cross Yosemite Creek on a bridge. About 500 feet beyond the bridge our signed route leaves the road and heads south again.

The forested trail is level for about ¾ mile, then crosses a dry streambed and begins climbing around a low granite ridge. Along this stretch Indian paintbrush, yarrow, penstemon, stonecrop and Mariposa lily delight the eye with their wild-flower colors. We soon surmount the ridge and descend over open granite, following ducks, to a junction with an alternate access trail (Lateral Trail #3) from the Tioga Road.

Moving south, we ford a small stream, near which camping is possible, and then we cut alternately toward and away from Yosemite Creek several times before the trail settles on a downward route beside the stream. Calm, beautiful pools in the eroded granite streambed tempt the swimmer to take a cool dip. Most of the campsites along the stream lack wood, and the least-used sites are east across the creek and not accessible when the water is high.

Chipmunks and golden-mantled ground squirrels scamper off under scattered Jeffrey pine, juniper and lodgepole pine as we stroll down this glaciated canyon, and robins, sapsuckers, juncos and hermit thrushes give avian flavor to the wildlife along this section of trail.

Bluejay Creek presents a tricky crossing during high water. The next stream is Eagle Peak Creek, and beyond the ford we go up this stream, leaving Yosemite Creek behind for a while. The trail to Eagle Peak (Lateral Trail #2) soon takes off to the west. It is well worth the hike, for it leads to one of the grandest of all views from the rim of Yosemite Valley.

Where we meet the North Dome Trail (see Day Hike #2), a granite shoulder separates us from Yosemite Creek. A short spur from this trail takes us to an overlook of Yosemite Falls. (Use due caution; one slip could be fatal.) A mile farther up this trail is Yosemite Point, where we find another superb panorama of the Yosemite country. These views of the top of the mighty *Cho-look,* or Yosemite Falls, the nearby Lost Arrow and the Valley itself provide unrivalled thrills.

From this junction our trail begins three miles of switchbacks down the north wall of Yosemite Valley, losing ½ mile of elevation as we drop quickly on granite sand. Upper Yosemite Falls remains out of sight behind a part of the Valley wall until we are well down the trail, but its roar is heard except late in the season, when the falls becomes a mere trickle or even dries up completely until the autumn rains begin. (A portion of the wall above this top section of trail broke loose in late 1980, unfortunately killing several hikers and wiping out a substantial section of trail. It was being rebuilt in 1982, and there may continue to be periodic closures in succeeding years as the work to restore the trail continues.)

From a viewpoint approximately level with the bottom of the upper falls, the trail swings upward toward the west under a cover of golden oak, incense-cedar, California bay and Douglas-fir. A number of springs appearing above the trail may be potable, but there's no guarantee. Note along here too that many of the trees have no branches on their upslope sides—evidence of natural (and unnatural) rockfalls from the walls above. Take care yourself not to dislodge any rocks that might tumble downslope and perhaps injure people where the trail switchbacks below. Finally, a last series of switchbacks under an oak canopy over loose granite gravel (*gruss*) brings us to the end of our hike at Sunnyside Camp on the Valley floor.

Day Hike #2   **North Dome**

Tioga Road to Yosemite Valley

11½ miles; net loss 4120′; total gain 1300′

Shuttle trip. G4.

This descending trail takes us from the Tioga Road to Yosemite Valley via the airy heights of North Dome above Tenaya Creek canyon. Backpackers may make the trip an overnighter with a stop near one of the streams along the way. Check on current regulations.

Our route initially follows the closed-off road to the closed Porcupine Creek Campground. In the westernmost part of this former camp our signed trail begins at Porcupine Creek. Our route takes off by crossing Porcupine Creek and heading gently uphill in a forest of lodgepole pine and red fir. The width of the trail hints that it has been used as a roadway in the past. On a fairly level pathway, we cross an intermittent stream and several wet meadows containing corn lilies before passing a lateral to the Snow Creek Trail (Day Hike #4).

A few yards beyond this junction the trail forks again. (The trail ahead—southwest, to the right—is shorter, but the traveler taking it misses the best part of this day hike: the trail to North Dome. The right-hand trail gradually descends the drainage of Lehamite Creek, through red-fir, white-fir and Jeffrey-pine forest and an occasional small, grassy meadow, to rejoin the North Dome trail just west of where the latter crosses Lehamite Creek.)

Choosing the North Dome route, we turn left at the second junction and climb in and out of several gullies through an open fir forest. Our route soon climbs toward a low ridgetop and just below it meets the signed ¼-mile lateral to Indian Ridge Natural Arch. It's well worth the slight detour to see this granite formation, for it is of a kind rarely seen in the Sierra. This natural bridge, or arch, was carved by wind and water, and it is a nice setting for photographs. Landmarks seen from the top of the rock include the Three Brothers, Sentinel Rock, Half Dome and the Clark Range.

Back on the main North Dome trail, we climb a few feet and then start a long descent along the granite spur of Indian Ridge toward North Dome, on the edge of Yosemite Valley. Half Dome looms larger and larger ahead across Tenaya canyon as we descend in open Jeffrey-pine and red-fir forest and cross glacially-smoothed granite slopes (watch for ducks) to the turnoff to North Dome.

The spur trail to North Dome drops steeply for a few hundred feet, then climbs gently to the broad summit. Watch carefully for the ducked route along here. Depending on air pollution, the view from the top can be exhilarating or disgusting. When it's clear, prospects are excellent of picking out many of the prominent points on the rim surrounding Yosemite Valley: Half Dome, within arm's reach, it seems (look for climbers on its face); Clouds Rest and Quarter Domes; Cathedral Rocks; Eagle Peak; and Illilouette Falls (till mid season). Jeffrey pines and huckleberry oaks struggle for survival here on the summit of the dome—a breezy spot to have lunch.

Back on the main trail, we follow a ducked course down the ridge nose over open granite and through dense huckleberry oak toward a crossing of Royal Arch Creek, which is dry in late season. Beyond the stream we cross a low ridge under pine and fir and arrive at Lehamite Creek, which is lined with willows, ferns and some extremely tall lupines. After a slight climb from this stream, we come to a junction with the shorter trail from Porcupine Creek and continue around the end of another low ridge to Indian Canyon Creek, where the air in midseason is fragrantly scented by flowering azaleas. From here the trail climbs again easily under red and white firs and some long-coned sugar pines, tops the next ridge and descends a few hundred feet to Yosemite Point, 3000 feet above the Valley floor.

Thundering Yosemite Falls can be heard but not seen a few hundred yards west. Directly below is the Park headquarters area, while down to the right is the Lost Arrow, a gigantic missilelike piece of granite, and one can see the Clark Range in the high country to the southeast.

The Yosemite Indians explained the origin of the Lost Arrow thus: The brave Kos-soo-kah went hunting the day before he and Tee-hee-neh were to be married. He said he'd shoot an arrow from the rim at the end of the day indicating to her the success of the hunt. However, he died in a rockslide from the rim while trying to fulfill his promise, so the gods lodged a column of rock—Hum-moo, or the Lost Arrow—between Yosemite Falls (Cho-look) and Lehamite Creek as a memorial to his faithfulness. Climbers may sometimes be observed doing a Tyrolean traverse between the rim and the Lost Arrow.

From Yosemite Point the trail continues down through Jeffrey pine, juniper and bush chinquapin on generally open, glaciated granite to a bridge over Yosemite Creek, where it is prudent to be careful *not* to get caught in the current and swept over the lip of the falls a few hundred yards away.

From Yosemite Creek we cross another shoulder of granite and pass a spur that leads to an outlook of Yosemite Falls itself before arriving at the Yosemite Creek trail, which we enjoy for the remaining 3 miles to the Valley floor (see Day Hike #1).

Day Hike #3 **Snow Creek Cascades**

Mirror Lake to Snow Creek Cascades

5½-mile loop; total gain 200'

F6.

This easy loop hike leads us to the cascades below Snow Creek Falls, past beautiful Mirror Lake/Meadow and through stands of very large old black oaks, Douglas-firs and incense-cedars.

From the shuttle-bus stop about a mile below Mirror Lake, step east a few yards onto the paved bridle path under the trees. Proceeding north under a heavy cover of Douglas-fir, incense-cedar, ponderosa pine and dogwood (one of the few tree species that lends some fall color to the Sierra scene), we soon arrive at a signed junction with the road bridge over Tenaya Creek and a trail to Indian Caves.

We stay on our horsey trail east of the creek and continue upstream, passing huge lichen-covered granite boulders which have weathered and fallen from the southwest ridge of Half Dome, thousands of feet above. About ¼ mile below Mirror Lake we take a trail to the left at a signed junction. After crossing Tenaya Creek on a footbridge, we walk the last few hundred yards on pavement to the southwest corner of Mirror Lake at the parking lot.

From the now unused parking lot a signed trail heads up Tenaya Creek canyon along the north side of Mirror Lake, which was formed by a rockslide across the stream in 1910. In early and mid season, if the lake is full after a wet winter and the air is still, reflections of the surrounding granite walls, forests and sky in the glassy surface of the lake give inspiration to even the least talented photographer and painter.

The lake, since its creation, has been gradually filling with sand brought down from the high country by Tenaya Creek, and would have filled in by now had not various measures, such as check dams upstream and a dam at the lake outlet, been used to delay this process. Until 1971 the sand was physically removed from the lake bottom by truck and loader during the fall when the lake was dry. But that unnatural practice has been stopped, and today you can observe the natural succession of Mirror Lake to Mirror Meadow.

The paved-then-oiled trail passes under a mixed cover of massive specimens of big-leaf maple, black oak, incense-cedar, Douglas-fir, canyon oak, ponderosa pine and bay tree, and actually enters *Hetch Hetchy* quadrangle just beyond Mirror Lake. We stroll along the level trail, accompanied by the calls of chickadees, Steller's jays and flickers, until we arrive at a fork. The Snow Creek trail (or Tenaya Lake and Tuolumne Meadows trail) branches left (Day Hike #4), but we move ahead another ½ mile to the unsigned spur trail up Snow Creek toward the cascades. This spur climbs among granite boulders under a dense cover of Douglas-fir, incense-cedar and bay trees along rushing Snow Creek. The well-defined route eventually fizzles out, and the more adventurous hiker may want to scramble up farther to eat lunch, meditate or snooze near the secluded pools below the actual falls. The falls themselves are accessible only to experienced rock climbers. There are trout visible in these pools but most are very small.

The loop trail continues by crossing Tenaya Creek on a sturdy wooden bridge and heading down the south side of the stream under the massive granite face of Half Dome looming more than 4000 feet overhead. Lush wet spots along the trail host typical water-loving plants: ferns, dogwoods, alders, azaleas and the primitive plants called horsetails. Here, as earlier on the walk, the most impressive plants are the huge black oaks, some over five feet in diameter and at least several hundred years old. Undoubtedly these very trees were a source of acorns for the Ahwahnechees who once had sole claim to the Valley.

The route of our return takes us by the east shore of shrinking Mirror Lake. Once we get to the footbridge below the lake, we can continue straight ahead, retracing our steps on the bridle path to the shuttle-bus stop, or we can cross to the abandoned Mirror Lake road and stroll along it to the Valley floor.

Day Hike #4   **Snow Creek Trail**

Yosemite Valley to Tioga Road

9 miles one way; net gain 4520$'$

Shuttle trip.

Labeled the Tenaya Lake and Tuolumne Meadows trail on the map, the Snow Creek trail is here described as it climbs from Mirror Lake in Yosemite Valley to the Tioga Road—a stiff ascent of over 4500 feet, or 500 feet average elevation gain per mile. For a description of this walk in the downhill direction, see *Yosemite National Park* by Schaffer.

The first 2 miles of this trail are described under Day Hike #3. At the fork ½ mile below Snow Creek cascades, we turn left off the cascades trail and immediately begin switchbacking up the granite walls of Tenaya canyon, amid golden oaks and black oaks. After several hundred feet of climbing we break out into more open cover of chaparral on granite slabs, where California fuchsia and mountain aster may be blooming until late season. Currants, azaleas and lupines compose the ground cover at numerous wet seeps along the trail.

Checking out the scenery during a rest stop on this well-engineered trail, one should be able to pick out Glacier Point and, below it, Monday Morning slab—a popular spot for beginning rock climbers to learn on. Half Dome, looming high above, makes a particularly photogenic subject in late-afternoon light. At the gap where the trail stops switchbacking and begins to level off, hikers escape the hot, open granite and chaparral for a cool cover of Jeffrey pines and red and white fir which was recently burned. Soon after leveling off we come to a junction near Snow Creek where Douglas squirrels are likely to be chattering irritatedly at our intrusion. This is a pleasant campsite for those wishing to spend several days doing this hike.

(The route directly ahead—obscured by the recent burn—is a lateral that connects this trail with the North Dome trail. It parallels Snow Creek about 100 feet above the water for 1¾ miles while climbing north. Where lively, bubbling Porcupine Creek cascades down over granite boulders and under a natural bridge toward Snow Creek, the trail turns left and climbs about 600 feet in the next mile to a junction with the Porcupine

Half Dome from the Snow Creek Trail

Creek/North Dome trail. From this junction a loop can be made back to the Valley via the North Dome and Yosemite Creek trails [Day Hikes #1 and #2].)

However, back at Snow Creek we proceed to the right, and after a hundred yards cross the creek on a bridge. Then we begin a gradual ascent away from the stream in a forest of lodgepole, sugar and Jeffrey pines with white fir. Alert hikers here may spot nuthatches, kinglets, nutcrackers, crow-sized pileated woodpeckers and even the uncommon black-backed, three-toed woodpecker among the many bird species living in this mixed conifer forest.

Our trail now climbs more steeply, and a series of switchbacks through trees mixed with chaparral bring us to a tributary of Snow Creek. A few yards beyond is a fork in the trail, and we go left, in the direction of May Lake.

(The trail to the right leads eventually to Tenaya Lake, 5½ miles away via Olmsted Point. It climbs steadily in mixed forest for about a mile, then breaks out into open montane chaparral consisting mainly of huckleberry oak and sagebrush high above Tenaya Creek. Quarter Domes, Clouds Rest and the many falls of the canyon below afford graphic illustrations of the grinding and carving power of the glaciers that once filled this canyon with ice nearly a mile thick [see the chapter "Geology"]. From here the route drops several hundred feet in brush before re-entering forest cover above a tributary of Tenaya Creek, where it resumes its climb toward Tenaya Lake and enters *Tuolumne Meadows* quadrangle.)

The main trail swings to the north high above Snow Creek and continues climbing in a forest interrupted by numerous open, grassy areas. As we gain the top of the ridge, the Tioga Road comes into view, and we can see Coyote Rocks in the northwest and Mt. Hoffmann ahead to the north. Useful as trail markers here are the orange license plates 10 feet up on trees, which indicate a winter travel route. Our trail rolls along in granite sand for ½ mile to the Tioga Road, meeting it at a

bend about ½ mile east of the May Lake road and just west of
a dead-end road to a borrow pit.

We can end our hike here (which necessitates a shuttle back
to the Valley), or the trek can be continued by crossing the
road and picking up the trail on the other side. It follows a
moranial ridge sparsely covered with red fir and western white
pine over huckleberry oak and pinemat manzanita. Crossing
over to the northwest side of the ridge on a heavily striated
section of glacially eroded granite bedrock. we note the Old
Tioga Road below heading north toward May Lake. Our route
here leaves *Hetch Hetchy* quadrangle, and leads to the May
Lake trail, which is described in the High Sierra Hiking Guide
to *Tuolumne Meadows* quadrangle.

Day Hike #5   **Lukens Lake**

White Wolf to Lukens Lake

2 miles one way; net gain 340′

E3.

This short trail is a very popular day hike to an oft-visited
and heavily fished lake near White Wolf. Those seeking solitude
had best make tracks on some other trail. Lukens Lake is,
however, an excellent hike for those who would like to sample
the uplands of Yosemite before deciding on a longer day hike
or backpack trip described in this guide. It is also a good intro-
duction to the backcountry for small children and elderly
people.

Our hike begins at the trailhead across the road from White
Wolf resort. The trail, which once ran directly across the
meadow, has been rerouted into the woods to avoid any more
damage to this fragile ecosystem. We pass a sign reminding us
No Pets are allowed on Park trails, and enter a stand of pole-
sized, snow-bent lodgepole pines. The lack of branches and

Right: Lukens Lake   *Thomas Winnett*

twigs on the ground is the result of scavenging by campers from the nearby White Wolf campground. Flowers of shooting star, knotweed, mountain aster and delphinium dot the ground, especially in the wetter spots. In drier areas, color is provided by pussy paws, lupine and streptanthus.

Our route crosses the Middle Fork Tuolumne River (here merely a small stream) on logs, and passes the trail to the Grand Canyon of the Tuolumne River (Backpack Trail #2). We continue climbing very gently under lodgepole pines near the stream to another junction, where a lateral (Lateral Trail #4) to the Ten Lakes trail forks left. Crossing a tributary stream on logs or rocks, we start climbing more steeply onto a glacial moraine in a forest of lodgepole pine and red fir. Golden-mantled ground squirrels are common along the trail, and a long, sloping meadow off to the right delights us with the color of bluebells, lupine, columbine and shooting stars. Just beyond a final little climb we come to a surprise view of the well-trampled shoreline of shallow Lukens Lake, where camping is not allowed. The lake contains rainbow trout, heavily fished.

(An alternative 1-mile route to the lake starts as a signed trailhead [map section E3] on the Tioga Road about 2 miles east of the turnoff to White Wolf. This route winds uphill ½ mile through a shady forest of red fir, western white pine and mountain hemlock to a saddle, then descends gently to the large meadow at the southeast end of Lukens Lake. The route to the right around the lake meets the trail from White Wolf.)

Day Hike #6   **Harden Lake**

White Wolf to Harden Lake
3 miles one way; net loss 340'

E3.

Harden Lake, like Lukens Lake (see Day Hike #5), is a nice place for those with limited time or ability to get at least a taste of the backcountry. However, solitude cannot be guaranteed—especially in mid season—and heavy fishing pressure is likely to curtail the number and size of fish any one angler catches.

Our route, a closed fire road, begins by heading north from White Wolf resort and soon bridges the infant Middle Tuolumne River, then parallels its sometimes splashing course down unglaciated granitic terrain. After a mile of easy descent, we pass a spur road to a sewage-treatment pond and then climb over a low ridge of glacial deposits before dipping into a shady alcove. Here at a junction we leave the road for a trail, which climbs gently around a ridge, first under lodgepole pines and then through a parklike stand of Jeffrey pines. In 2/3 mile the trail ends and we follow Harden Lake road across relatively flat glacial sediments. In a few minutes we reach a gravelly junction with a trail to Pate Valley and take it to the southeast corner of Harden Lake.

Harden Lake is formed by meltwater and rainwater dammed behind a moraine left by the last glaciation. It has no permanent inlet or outlet stream. It is, moreover, quite shallow, and its rainbow-trout population is heavily fished. Opportunities are good for observing water-associated insect life here, particularly dragonflies, damsel-flies and water boatmen. No camping is permitted.

(Beyond Harden Lake this trail continues north and east down into the Grand Canyon of the Tuolumne. It drops steeply, switchbacking through fine, lush groves of aspens and willows before joining the trail from White Wolf to Pate Valley in a stand of black oak, incense-cedar, white fir and Jeffrey pine (Backpack Trail #2].)

Day Hike #7   **Tamarack Creek**

Tioga Road to Tamarack Flat Campground

2½ miles one way; net loss 440$'$

Shuttle trip. C5.

The trail described here is a segment of an old route that once was an important connection between Yosemite Valley and Mather Ranger Station. Today it is infrequently maintained and is mainly of interest to anglers after the abundant trout in the pools of Tamarack Creek.

We begin at a small parking area on the south side of the Tioga Road about 2½ miles east of Gin Flat. Our signed route descends gently under a heavy cover of red and white fir (notice the differences in bark coloration), and we soon pass along the east side of a meadow with shoulder-high lupines on its margin. Ducks should guide you here. Re-entering timber, we have to crawl over some windfall (in late 1982) before crossing a tributary and finally arriving at gurgling Tamarack Creek itself. An old "T" blaze may be seen on a lodgepole pine on this section of trail.

We cross another tributary, and the windfall continues to be heavy as we maintain our gradual descent beside the trout-filled pools of Tamarack Creek. Also evident to the alert hiker along this stretch of trail are such typical forest birds as brown creepers, ruby-crowned kinglets, yellow-rumped warblers and mountain chickadees.

Our route gradually levels out in open lodgepole pine and red fir before arriving at Tamarack Flat Campground near Site #1. For a description of the route down the Old Big Oak Flat Road to Yosemite Valley, see Schaffer's *Yosemite National Park*.

(A continuation of this trail *north* of the Tioga Road from the trailhead starts a few yards to the east at a sign on the other side of the road. This segment drops steadily in mixed timber toward Aspen Valley, Mather Ranger Station and Hetch Hetchy Reservoir. It was covered with considerable fallen timber in late 1982 and was apparently overdue for maintenance work. Since it continues off the edge of *Hetch Hetchy* quadrangle, it is described in Schaffer's book.)

Backpack Trail #1   **Ten Lakes Trail**

Tioga Road to Ten Lakes

6½ miles one way to first lake; net gain 1520′; total gain 2120′

F3.

The Ten Lakes trail, one of the more popular backpack routes in Yosemite National Park, is beginning to show the marks of overuse: deeply rutted multilane tracks, lack of firewood, piles of garbage around the lakes. One hopes hikers will all come to understand what thoughtlessness and just plain numbers of feet can do to this fragile high country, which has less than a three-month growing season during which to heal its bruises. Ten Lakes justly deserves its popularity: it is an extremely scenic area, less than four hours from the road, with six *readily accessible* lakes in about a two-square-mile area. Please don't let success spoil it!

The trailhead is on the Tioga Road a hundred feet west of Yosemite Creek at the west end of the parking lot on the north side of the road. We head west about 1/10 mile to a junction where we turn right and take off north on the level in lodgepole pine and red fir. The route soon begins to climb over open granite dotted with Jeffrey pine and Sierra juniper, following ducks where there is no obvious trail. Sandy pockets in the granite slabs collect enough moisture to nourish three-petaled Mariposa lilies, Indian paintbrush, and a thick-leaved succulent plant called stonecrop. The broad valley of Yosemite

Creek stretches below to the east, and Mt. Hoffmann rises sharply on its east rim. Polish on the rocks and glacial erratics here are evidence that powerful glaciers once filled this valley with ice.

Beyond the slabs we re-enter forest and follow a gently ascending duff trail through lodgepole pine and red fir, where pussy paws, yarrow milfoil and paintbrush add their hues to the ground cover. We jump across an intermittent stream (not shown on the map), pass the lateral to White Wolf (Lateral Trail #4) and then jump the all-year stream that is on the map.

Our trail, under lodgepole and fir, gradually ascends for 1½ miles and then crosses several branches of a small stream. At the crossings, water-loving pink shooting stars and tall, white-flowered corn lilies keep their feet wet. Next we begin to climb steeply, north of a creek flowing down from Half Moon Meadow. Western white pine makes its appearance as we descend slightly to the south side of Half Moon Meadow.

From the meadow we climb once again, this time switch-backing steeply up through open lodgepole forest that grades into sagebrush before we come to a trail junction. Lower Grant Lake lies 1 mile south (see Lateral Trail #1). We move north across the open ridgetop, where wind-beaten, low-lying speci-mens of timberline-tree species—lodgepole pine and mountain hemlock—are scattered about in little groups. Having left the watershed of the Merced River for that of the Tuolumne, we switchback steeply down toward Ten Lakes, and first one and then another of the lakes comes into view. Despite the name "Ten Lakes," there are really only seven of any size, some of them are not visible from the trail, and only six are easily reached.

Where the route levels off in mountain hemlock and lodge-pole pine, we come to one sign of overuse: a proliferation of trails. The first one before the stream leads to campsites on the north shore of the first lake. Just across the stream is an un-marked and unmaintained trail to the right, which leads to the

Ten Lakes Basin

upper two Ten Lakes, via the east shore of the first lake. Down-hill and to the left are the other two of the five westerly lakes. The two easternmost lakes are straight ahead, separated from the others by about a mile of trail (see below).

For the upper lakes here, take the right fork and climb a few hundred yards to the lowest of the three lakes above the main trail. It is heavily used, and there is essentially no firewood. There are, however, good campsites all around the lake. Its rainbow and brook trout are heavily fished.

The second lake of this trio is reached by climbing up the trail beside its cascading outlet, first in a forest of hemlock and lodgepole, then across some granite boulders being slowly overgrown by elderberry bushes. This rocky lake has good campsites near the outlet and at the inlet where the trail ends. Wood is ample. The rainbow and brook trout population is fished heavily, mostly by anglers coming up from the lower lake.

The highest lake of this group, another ½ mile upstream, is mosquitoey later into the season than the lower lakes. It appears to be the deepest and least camped and fished of the three, with campsites near the outlet. It is reached by continuing cross-country up the left side of the stream flowing out of it down to the second lake.

Back at the main trail junction below, by going downhill we soon reach the shore of the largest of the westerly five lakes of the group. Many campsites are located around the lake, and there are some nice islands to swim to. Wood is scarce, and the population of rainbow and brook trout is heavily fished all summer.

The northernmost lake of these five is the hardest to get to, and hence the most secluded, but it still has its complement of litter. It is reached by a trail around the west side of the large lake and a short climb over the ridge north of it. The best camping is at the north end east of the outlet. Firewood is scarce and fishing pressure for rainbow and brook trout is moderate.

The route to the eastern two Ten Lakes continues east from the southwest corner of the largest of these westerly Ten Lakes. Our trail passes through several wet meadows and climbs northeast on mica-rich granite toward the summit of Grand Mountain. The high country near Mts. Conness and Dana in the east and Sawtooth Ridge in the northeast comes into view as we swing south and descend a bit, cross the outlet of and arrive at the north shore of the larger lake of the easterly Ten Lakes group.

The better campsites lie on the west and north sides of this lake, where wood is ample. The population of rainbow trout gets only moderate fishing pressure. (The most remote of the seven Ten Lakes is a mile north and 400 feet in elevation below this one by off-trail travel.) From this last lake on the trail, our path goes by a small pond, and begins to drop steadily toward the gorge of Cathedral Creek. We enter the *Tuolumne Meadows* quadrangle about where we ford a streamlet not shown on the map, and the trail from here is described in the High Sierra Hiking Guide to that quadrangle.

Backpack Trail #2
Grand Canyon of the Tuolumne
White Wolf to Muir Gorge
18 miles one way; net loss 3450′; total gain 1680′
E3.

A round trip on this backpack trail requires a minimum of three days' walking—more if you continue up the river to Tuolumne Meadows. From White Wolf (7850′), the trail descends to Pate Valley (4400′) and then climbs up the Grand Canyon of the Tuolumne around Muir Gorge to map's edge opposite Cathedral Creek (5600′). This long jaunt takes one into the depths of a canyon deeper than Yosemite Valley along

a free and wild river where unexcelled campsites lie near emer-
ald pools and blue cascades. The hike out from Pate Valley is
not easy, but to those who experience this remaining wild portion of a great river, now drowned along much of its length by
dead reservoirs, it is worth the sweat.

From White Wolf we follow the Lukens Lake trail (Day Hike
#5) about a mile, to the first junction. Here we turn left and
head north for the Tuolumne River. Our route is quite level,
and since the walking is easy under lodgepole pines being succeeded by red firs, we have time to note signs of black bear
in the area: droppings on the trail, scratched tree trunks,
tracks on the path. Smaller animals one might see include
dark-eyed juncos feeding on the ground, and hairy woodpeckers, red-and-yellow western tanagers and brownish-red
pine grosbeaks in the trees. The hermit thrush's melodious
tunes fill this forest in mid season.

As the trail loses elevation red fir becomes abundant, then
gives way to western white pine, Jeffrey pine and white fir.
When the upper end of Hetch Hetchy Reservoir comes into
sight, incense-cedar, black oak and manzanita start to appear.
Meeting the trail between Pate Valley and Harden Lake (Day
Hike #6) we turn right onto it.

The next part of our long descent takes us past several wet
seeps and springs flowing out of the canyon wall which are
overgrown by such moisture-loving species as alder, dogwood,
willow, Sierra lily and cranesbill. After a stretch of relatively
gentle downhill in forest, we begin a long series of switchbacks,
following Morrison Creek for a while as it tumbles toward the
river. There are some possibilities for emergency camping along
this stream.

The trail crosses Morrison Creek on rocks, then switchbacks
down through oak woods, open granite and chaparral. Vistas
up and down the canyon and across it to Rancheria Mountain
and the cascades of Piute Creek open up as the vegetation thins
out. It is wise, when returning from the river, to do this part of

the trail either early or late in the day because of the midday heat. We jump across a welcome unnamed stream (and potential bivouac site) and continue our switchbacking descent as we pass around a vernal pool ringed with various kinds of wildflowers along its shrinking shoreline.

After this we switchback down again toward the river in a forest of black oak, incense-cedar and ponderosa pine. This is rattlesnake country, and hikers should be aware that rattlers blend in very well with dead leaves. They are able to climb trees, but do not do so very well, and occasionally fall to the ground at the oddest moments. It must be emphatically stated that rattlesnakes are usually more afraid of us than we are of them. Every rattler the author has seen has been going the other way if it could. They are a natural, though potentially dangerous, part of this ecosystem and should be treated with respect, but not with fear or hatred.

After the trail levels off near the river, camps can be made from here on upstream; wood is usually plentiful, and the water is deep and cold until late season. High air temperatures, however, can be a problem from early June on as can face-loving gnats—which seem to replace mosquitoes as insect pests when the latter go out of season.

Two successive bridges take the trail across the Tuolumne River to the Pate Valley side, where there is a shady camping area under a heavy cover of ponderosa pine and incense-cedar. The bears here are *very* smart, so absolutely *no* food should be left unattended—even during the day—unless it is properly suspended out of their reach (see the chapter "Fauna").

Beyond the campground at a fork, the left branch leads to Rodgers Lake and Pleasant Valley (Backpack Trails #3 and #4), and we go right (east) toward Muir Gorge.

On the floor of the valley, we walk along under a dense cover of ponderosa pine shading young incense-cedar trees, which are evidence of the passage of much time since the last forest fire here. However, when one does occur, the large accumulation of limbs, needles and other debris on the ground will make it a very hot blaze indeed. (There was also heavy windfall on the trail in late 1982.) Preventive burns are being carried out in Yosemite Valley for this very reason, but the likelihood of that type of treatment here at Pate is remote.

Coming out of the woods, our route goes right along (or *in,* during high water) the Tuolumne for a while on cemented boulder tread. Next the trail climbs high above the river, drops down beside it for a while, then climbs again, reflecting the difficulty of constructing a route along a torrential stream in a gorge. In the forested stretches beside the water, hikers may encounter band-tailed pigeons, blue grouse, robins and gray squirrels, and such reptiles as fence lizards and rattlesnakes. Along the high, open granite stretches, one can absorb the geological lessons inscribed in the tall, glacier-carved canyon walls and the hanging valleys. There are several beautiful campsites beside the deep pools along this stretch of the river.

(When we reach the lower end of Muir Gorge, the trail climbs about 800 feet up and *around the gorge.* It redescends to the river about 1 mile above where it left it. There is no trail through Muir Gorge itself. Only experienced backpackers who can swim well and use climbing rope should attempt to negotiate this part of the canyon, and only during *low water.* There are several campsites near tributary streams—one has a splendid waterfall—as the long detour begins.)

The trail climbs up under tree cover, crossing Rodgers Canyon creek on a bridge and Register Creek below its falls on a rock ford. Then it breaks out into the open, switchbacking high above Muir Gorge onto a glacially polished granite knob. Soon the trail descends back into the canyon, dropping steeply down a gully choked with incense-cedar, black oak and white fir. Across the canyon, Ten Lakes creek is obscured by scrub and fallen rock.

We resume our trek up the canyon, passing some excellent examples of *roches moutonnées,* house-sized and larger bedrock outcroppings ground by glaciers so that their "upstream" surfaces are gently sloping while their "downstream" faces are nearly vertical, having been plucked at by the moving ice. Acorn-eating California gray and California ground squirrels are abundant in the canyon, along with band-tailed pigeons, flickers and Steller's jays. Again, hikers should be alert for rattlesnakes along the trail.

As we approach the cascades of Cathedral Creek (and map's edge), we are among huge talus blocks under pine, oak, fir and incense-cedar, with wild cherry, elderberry and azalea bushes below the tree canopy. From here the trail is described in the High Sierra Hiking Guide to *Tuolumne Meadows*.

Backpack Trail #3   **Rodgers Lake**

White Wolf to Rodgers Lake

21 miles one way; net gain 1660′; total gain 5620′

Rodgers Lake is a large subalpine lake in the *Tuolumne Meadows* quadrangle just off the northeast corner of the *Hetch Hetchy* quad. The lake is lightly used because the hike to it takes two days or more, including a long descent to the bottom of the Grand Canyon of the Tuolumne River and a long ascent out of it. The rewards of solitude and rugged alpine beauty await those who make the long trek in.

The first 10 miles of the Rodgers Lake hike are included in the description of Backpack Trail #2. At Pate Valley (map section F2) our trail branches from the Muir Gorge trail and soon begins its 1-mile vertical ascent in 11 miles to Rodgers Lake, an essentially unbroken climb except for a few miles of level trail in Rodgers Canyon. Do not make this climb during the middle of a summer's day unless you're really tough. The slope faces southwest, so it is sunny and hot, and there is only one reliable water source—5 miles uphill—before Rodgers Canyon.

From the Tuolumne River trail we climb a few hundred feet
up an open, grassy slope—parched and brown by midseason—
and then enter what turns out to be nearly continuous tree
cover for the next 5 miles. Our trail parallels Piute Creek,
which is off to the left under a canopy of incense-cedar, golden
and black oak and ponderosa pine. After a mile we start
switchbacking away from the stream up the canyon wall to the
east. At occasional wet spots one sees California Sister butterflies—brown except for a white stripe and a bright orange spot
on each wing. There has been all too much switchback cutting
by people coming down the trail here. Not only is this practice ugly, but it makes erosion worse, destroys plant life and
increases trail-maintenance costs.

Higher up this long series of switchbacks, we get into some
uncommon volcanic mudflow deposits and begin to meet Jeffrey pine, juniper and, in wet spots, aspen. Pleasant wildflower
color is provided by many species along the trail, including
paintbrush, yarrow, Mariposa lily, mule ears, columbine, cow-
parsnip and farewell-to-spring. At the junction with the Pleasant Valley trail (Backpack Trail #4) our route continues
climbing to the right (southeast). This junction is a lovely spot
to eat lunch, with an open patch of lush green grass circled by
trembling aspens and young juniper trees, where one is likely
to hear and see western tanagers, black-headed grosbeaks,
wrens, hummingbirds and flycatchers in midseason. For water,
a small cold, unmapped spring-fed stream up the trail about
100 yards ahead flows at least until midseason.

We continue steep climbing for another ½ mile over more
volcanic mudflows; then the trail becomes gentler under scattered lodgepole, aspen, white fir, Jeffrey pine and big junipers—
and even goes downhill for a while. Watch for red-capped chip-
ping sparrows along this stretch of trail. Some of the high
country above Tuolumne Meadows comes into view to the
east as we resume climbing. Then we hear the stream in
Rodgers Canyon, and finally it comes into view alongside the
trail. There is a fair campsite here with views across the Grand

Canyon of the Tuolumne River toward Ten Lakes.

From this campsite the trail climbs away from the stream onto open glacially polished granite up neatly constructed stairs, and we pass through a stand of large, dead lodgepole pines—probably the result of a lodgepole-needle-miner outbreak in decades past. Needle-miners are the larvae of moths that defoliate lodgepole pines by tunneling in the needles, eating and killing them. (There's a good example of the work of this insect above Tenaya Lake along the Tioga Road.)

Rodgers Meadow is next along the trail. The turf here is thick and lush, dwarf huckleberry abounds—and there are mosquitoes. During July, from here on up to Rodgers Lake the insects are almost intolerable, so be sure to have plenty of insect repellent. Anything high in N, N-diethyl-meta-toluamide works (over 25%).

The spotted sandpiper, an amazing bird, may be found here in the meadows most of the summer. This bird ranges from sea level to alpine lakes, from Alaska to Argentina, wherever there is water. And those gray mammals in the meadow are Belding's ground squirrels, a common, burrow-building rodent at this elevation.

At the upper end of the meadow we pass a packer campsite off to the left of the trail and re-enter timber, splashing across Rodgers Canyon creek twice before coming to a junction. The trail that goes straight ahead is described later as an alternate return route from Rodgers Lake. But now we go right, paralleling the creek and climbing again, this time in a subalpine forest of mountain hemlock, lodgepole pine and western white pine. The common white-flowered shrub here is Labrador tea, an indicator of a cool, wet microclimate. Why anyone would use it to make tea is a mystery; its leaves smell like turpentine!

Where we meet the outlet of Neall Lake at a junction, we are less than 0.1 mile from the lake, which is thick with mosquitoes well into late season. Camping is best near the outlet at this lovely lake.

We continue on in granite sand and steps up the steep down-canyon side of a *roche moutonnée* toward Rodgers Lake, entering *Tuolumne Meadows* quadrangle just above Neall Lake. We soon reach beautiful Rodgers Lake itself, in a striking sub-alpine setting. Regulation Peak immediately to the south makes a perfect backdrop for this pristine body of water. The lake curves around Regulation Peak in a nearly 90° arc, and there are numerous possible campsites near its convoluted shores. Firewood is scarce, though stands of lodgepole pine, mountain hemlock and whitebark pine are found around the lake. Its population of rainbow trout is lightly fished.

An alternate return route to Rodgers Meadow continues around Rodgers Lake and climbs to a divide where one has good views of the diking in the south ridge of Volunteer Peak and of the country toward Tower Peak in the north. From the divide we drop steeply north through wet meadows covered with heather, willow and mountain hemlock, enter *Matterhorn Peak* quad, and reach a junction with the Tahoe-Yosemite and Pacific Crest trails.

From this junction we travel west on the Tahoe-Yosemite Pacific Crest Trail about ½ mile to another junction, where we leave it and head southwest—walking in *Tower Peak* quadrangle for a few hundred yards. The trail passes Murdock Lake and meadows, where robins and dark-eyed juncos may be sighted. Beyond Murdock, our path begins dropping on granite sand under lodgepole pines toward Rodgers Meadow. After re-entering *Hetch Hetchy* quadrangle, we pass a cold, spring-fed streamlet before rejoining the trail to Pate Valley.

Left: **Rodgers Meadow**

Backpack Trail #4   **Pleasant Valley**

White Wolf to Pleasant Valley

18 miles one way; net loss 1120′; total gain 3980′

F1.

Pleasant Valley is a small, forested flat on Piute Creek which offers quiet seclusion in a sort of mini-Yosemite-Valley setting.

The first and middle portions of the hike to Pleasant Valley from White Wolf are covered in Backpack Trails #2 and #3. At the junction (map section F1) five miles north of Pate Valley we turn left and continue climbing north toward Pleasant Valley. The canyonside is lightly forested with lodgepole pines, white firs and large old junipers, shading an understory of huckleberry oak, Queen Anne's lace, paintbrush, marigolds, whiteheads, asters, columbines and lupines. At numerous wet spots along the trail, Acmon blue butterflies congregate to wet their whistles. Our path swings in and out of little gullies and soon begins to drop steadily toward Pleasant Valley. Irwin Bright and Table lakes are visible in the valley ahead as we switchback down on dark, fine-grained igneous rock.

When we reach the valley of Table Lake, a rank growth of willows, aspen, dogwood and eight-foot-tall (!) delphiniums closes in over our heads. An old trail to Irwin Bright and Table lakes used to branch off along this piece of trail, but it no longer exists—it has been recycled by nature! We continue westward, crossing several open ridges with water-filled depressions between them. The dark igneous rocks here are sparsely covered with spiraea, honeysuckle, juniper and some pine and fir.

After the trail rounds a shoulder, we pass through an old stock gate into Pleasant Valley. Our route soon reaches Piute Creek and we cross on logs upstream from the ford. (The faint trail going up the east side of the creek leads nowhere.) Beyond the crossing there's a signed junction, the right branch

Left: Rodgers Lake, looking west   *NPS*

Rancheria Falls

leading to a campsite below a series of cascades on Piute Creek. (The trail to the left is described as Backpack Trail #5.) The campsite upstream is a typical packer site, with tables and chairs and hitching rails for the stock—a nice, quiet spot *if* you get there first. And the swimming is great. If this spot is already taken, nice camps can be made elsewhere in the valley along Piute Creek. No matter where you camp in this area, be *sure* you secure your food from the bears.

Backpack Trail #5   **Pleasant Valley**

Hetch Hetchy to Pleasant Valley

18½ miles one way; net gain 3040′; total gain 5770′

B2.

This is a possible alternate route into the back country north of the Grand Canyon of the Tuolumne River when access to the usual trailheads at White Wolf and Tuolumne Meadows is still blocked by late-melting winter snow along the Tioga Road. The trail is hot and dry during most of the summer, but there are two fairly reliable watercourses along the route—Rancheria Creek and an unnamed stream originating on the north side of Rancheria Mountain—and hikers willing to give up high-country scenery in return for seclusion and an absence of mosquitoes will like this trail for mid- and late-season trips as well.

From O'Shaughnessy Dam in the *Lake Eleanor* quadrangle, we take the Lake Vernon/Tiltill Valley Trail (Backpack Trail #7) to the junction before Rancheria Falls. Our route ahead drops on cobbled rock to a bridge over fast-flowing Rancheria Creek and then begins to climb steeply on well-engineered switchbacks over granite through a sparse cover of golden oak with manzanita. Looking north from the ridge beyond Rancheria Creek toward Tiltill Valley, hikers with really good eyes or with binoculars who are familiar with the single-leaf pinyon pine may be able to spot a stand of these trees. They are generally globular in shape, with shorter needles than the associated Digger pines. The largest pinyon pine yet measured in California stands in this grove—a rather surprising record since pinyon pines are common in the eastern desert mountains of California but rare on the western Sierra slopes.

The steep switchbacks end north of Le Conte Point, but the trail keeps climbing in cover that alternates between chaparral and forest. We pass through a series of burns where wild cherry, whitethorn and manzanita thrive in this disturbed habitat. Such wildflowers as yarrow milfoil, penstemon, lupine, buckwheat, paintbrush and wild strawberry also do well in burned-over areas like these.

We continue climbing steadily for several miles, high above the Grand Canyon of the Tuolumne River in incense-cedar, white-fir and Jeffrey-pine forest. Finally, to the gurgle of moving water, we come out of the forest into a clearing at a most welcome stream flowing off Rancheria Mountain.

There is a nice campsite here, and firewood is abundant. After a refreshing interlude at this welcome waterway, we resume hiking toward the northeast in open fir forest beside a branch of the creek and pass through a series of meadows containing a myriad of colorful plants: blue lupine, orange paintbrush, yellow mule ears, scarlet gilia, and tall violet delphinium. We recross the unnamed stream to the north, its margins dense with monkey flower, cranesbill and rein orchids.

After the trail, on volcanic deposits here, passes close beneath the summit of Rancheria Mountain in open forest, we begin a long descent toward Pleasant Valley on the northwest side of the ridge high above Breeze Creek. The path switchbacks down in red and white fir to a saddle, where it forks. Pleasant Valley is 2 miles downhill to the east.

(The trail to the north climbs, in places very steeply, to a series of ponds that are very quiet and are teeming with wildlife: water boatmen, damselflies, water striders, frogs and even, occasionally, ducks, with olive-sided flycatchers overhead. There are possibilities for rather uninspiring camping here, and firewood is abundant. Campers should be especially careful, though, about fouling the water in old, shallow ponds like these because the lack of flow increases the effect of even small amounts of pollutants. Beyond these ponds, the trail climbs to a stream crossing and enters *Tower Peak* quadrangle.)

From the saddle, our trail drops very steeply on volcanic mudflow deposits toward Pleasant Valley. There is again evidence of past forest fires, as on other sections of this trail, and we see here midsuccessional species which thrive after fires, such as gooseberry, deer brush and bracken, with some aspen and willows in the wetter spots. At the end of our switchbacking descent we enter flat-bottomed Pleasant Valley, dotted with groves of aspen and clumps of willow in a lush grass cover, and cross a usually dry streambed. At a fork the trail to Pate Valley and White Wolf goes right (see Backpack Trails #2, #3 and #4), and we continue ahead to the main established campsite beside cascading Piute Creek. Wood is scarce at the campsite. If it is already occupied, good spots can be found elsewhere on the stream. Campers should be sure to secure their food against hungry bears if they wish to avoid hunger pangs themselves (see the chapter "Fauna").

Backpack Trail #6   **Lake Vernon**

Hetch Hetchy to Lake Vernon via Beehive

11 miles one way; net gain 2720′; total gain 3200′

B2.

This is the shorter of two routes into Lake Vernon from Hetch Hetchy Reservoir, and it is recommended for those who have just a two-day weekend and for hikes during the hottest part of the summer in order to avoid the blistering route in via

Tiltill Valley. It also offers a taste of high-country, glaciated landscapes earlier and later in the year than do trails with trailheads in the higher elevations of Yosemite National Park.

To begin, we cross O'Shaughnessy Dam and go through the tunnel on Lake Eleanor Road to the north side of the reservoir. Vegetation here is that typical of lower elevations in the Sierra, big-leaf maple, golden and black oaks and Digger pines being the predominant trees with yerba santa, poison-oak, manzanita and wild cherry among the shrubs. Where the trail to Tiltill Valley and Pleasant Valley branches right (see Backpack Trails #7 and #5), we stay on the now-abandoned road, which is being recycled into trail.

This former road switchbacks up for about two miles through open foothill woodland where California ground squirrels can be seen gathering acorns in late season. At the top of this part of the climb we leave the old road to Lake Eleanor and take a signed trail to the right into a forest cover that has changed with elevation, now being mostly incense-cedar, ponderosa pine and sugar pine.

Our path leads us gently up dry, dusty switchbacks on granite-sand (*gruss*) footing through recently burned chaparral and mixed evergreen forest inhabited by such birds as Steller's jays, downy woodpeckers, nuthatches, dark-eyed juncos and robins. One might also be fortunate enough to spot the uncommon white-headed woodpecker drumming on an insect-infested tree. We pass a small pond on our left which is dry in late season—a classic textbook example of hydrarch succession—the gradual change with time from a pond to a forest.

At the next two junctions with trails to Laurel Lake (see Schaffer's *Yosemite National Park*) we keep to the right. The second junction is at Beehive, a meadow with a snow-measuring marker out in the middle. The metal markers on trailside trees coming in from the old Lake Eleanor road sometimes guide snow surveyors here in the winter. Camping is possible here since the spring in the meadow flows at least until late summer.

From Beehive we continue steadily upward, now in pine-and-fir forest, with Douglas squirrels and mountain chickadees chattering and calling in the trees. Our trail forks again, this time at the end of Moraine Ridge, and we go right here too, dropping first in burned forest then onto open, polished granite above Falls Creek. Watch for ducks and lines of rocks marking the route here on the exposed rock. Nature has left an interesting geological legacy along this section of trail: red, iron-stained glacial polish. It is worth tarrying here a few minutes to observe this phenomenon (see the chapter "Geology").

Falls Creek below Lake Vernon

Our trail now climbs across a low ridge and drops to a junction 0.1 mile below Lake Vernon. To the east are Falls Creek and Tiltill Valley (see Backpack Trail #7). Here we continue north in Jeffrey pine and lodgepole pine toward the lake, where east of the trail there are many possible campsites with fine views. Wood is somewhat scarce, and the lake's rainbow-trout population is fished heavily all summer. This trail finally peters out north of the lake, where there are good campsites on Falls Creek.

Backpack Trail #7   **Lake Vernon**

Hetch Hetchy to Lake Vernon via Tiltill Valley
16 miles one way; net gain 2720′; total gain 4810′
B2.

This route to Lake Vernon is recommended only for early- or very-late-season travel, because the climb from Hetch Hetchy to the ridge above Tiltill Valley is extremely hot and tedious, and there is little water between Rancheria Creek and Lake Vernon during August and September. The trail in via Beehive (Backpack Trail #6) is a better route, especially during mid to late season.

Our trail begins at O'Shaughnessy Dam, which backs the Tuolumne River up a canyon that once rivaled the grandeur of Yosemite (see the chapter "History") and forms Hetch Hetchy Reservoir. We cross the dam and hike through the tunnel to the north side of the lake along the old Lake Eleanor road. Typical foothill vegetation of Digger pine, California bay, canyon (golden) oaks, yerba santa and poison-oak covers the hillside, where as early as June the grass turns dry and brown.

After a mile on the road, we branch right at a signed junction onto the trail heading east toward Wapama Falls, which pours water into the reservoir all year. During winter and spring, another falls, Tueeulala, drops lacily over the sheer cliff west of Wapama. Spectacular Kolana Rock is prominent across the reservoir, and Hetch Hetchy Dome rises on our left above its drowned base.

Falls Creek is a reliable source of water, and it's a good idea to carry some from here, especially late in the season—although to be safe you should boil it. White-throated swifts whiz by overhead, and several species of reptile, including the low-slung alligator lizard, rustle through the litter under manzanita scrub as we climb steadily through dry foothill woodland, characterized by golden oak trees here. Unfortunately gnats are also here, and they are especially pesky in late season.

Tueeulala and Wapama falls

After we actually enter *Hetch Hetchy* quadrangle, the trail curves north and drops to a bridged crossing of Tiltill Creek. A short mile beyond Tiltill Creek the trail forks. To the right are Rancheria Creek and Pleasant Valley (see Backpack Trail #5). We take the left fork toward Tiltill Valley and Lake Vernon, and immediately begin a long series of hot, dry switchbacks up a chaparral-covered slope. A few shade-giving Digger pines and black and golden oaks are mercifully spaced along the path. As we trudge upward, ponderosa pines begin to appear, and at our feet wild strawberry, yarrow milfoil, farewell-to-spring and brodiaea flowers make the slogging more bearable.

We eventually gain a summit of sorts below peak 6395 and pass a water-lily-covered pond that has the rather uncommon Washington lily growing on its margins. This plant with large, showy, white flowers and long, linear leaves grows to six feet tall. Passing through a much moister habitat now, in alder, aspen, thimbleberry, dogwood and sweet-smelling azaleas, we soon drop a few hundred feet into Tiltill Valley. The trailbed across the meadow has been re-engineered, and should be less mucky than it used to be.

Tiltill Valley is a happy hangout for bears, especially if the berry crop is a good one. Even if it's not, they'll still be more than willing to relieve campers of any food not ingeniously secured from them (see the chapter "Fauna"). Out in the meadow, the trail forks. We'll be taking the left fork to Lake Vernon.

(The right branch here goes east up the meadow and then starts to climb north out of the valley through a cover of incense-cedars and black and golden oaks, which soon gives way to hot, dry, dusty chaparral. When this trail was built, it must have been fashionable to go *diretissima* (straight up) rather than switchbacking reasonably. Stopping for breath and shade, the hiker may see through his sweat-stung eyes a variety of birds that seem to be remarkably contented here on this hot, dry slope: band-tailed pigeons, flickers, Steller's jays and blue grouse [the males usually heard only, "booming" in mid-season, while females with young are often seen around here later in the summer]. We do get some nice views back toward Tiltill Valley and Hetch Hetchy as well as Rancheria Creek [Deep Canyon on the topo] to the east. The trail finally levels off somewhat near map's edge and then enters the *Tower Peak* quadrangle in a forest of lodgepole pine and red fir.)

From the junction we continue left on the main trail along the northern edge of the marshy upper meadow of Tiltill Valley through tall bracken and grasses. Redwinged blackbirds can be heard singing ("ook-a-lee") out in the wetter parts of the meadow, though this bird is actually much more common in the lowlands than in the Sierra. We cross Tiltill Creek at a stand of maple and incense-cedar and pass by some choice campsites at the upper end of the lower meadow. A series of bedrock mortar sites lie across the creek near some very gnarled and old black-oak trees, no doubt a source of acorns-to-grind long ago for the Ahwahnechees before their destruction by the white man.

The trail makes a sharp right turn just as it enters the meadow beyond Tiltill Creek and starts a long climb to the divide above Lake Vernon. As we switchback up in pine forest, several miles of charred trunks and snags of Jeffrey pine with a dense undergrowth of incense-cedar and red fir seedlings and whitethorn scrub (scratchy on bare legs!) tell us that a large fire here in the past decade or so set succession back from dense forest to a sparse cover of scattered trees and dense shrubs. Birds do well here, though, and the knowledgeable hiker will note lazuli buntings, mountain quail, phoebes, olive-sided flycatchers, fox sparrows and rufous-sided towhees in shrublands off the trail. Many of our loveliest mountain wildflowers do best in this open type of habitat too; especially abundant along the trail here are forget-me-not (and its stick-to-wool-socks seeds), nightshade, gilia, penstemon and, in wetter spots, wild onion, corn lily, cranesbill, rein-orchid and cow parsnip. After rounding a meadow, the trail finally leaves whitethorn scrub and scattered, charred trees and turns north on nearly level ground under red fir. We encounter our first water since Tiltill Creek, an unnamed stream flowing off Mount Gibson, and then make a series of switchbacks down open granite toward Lake Vernon, at the bottom of the broad, glaciated valley of Falls Creek.

Lake Vernon is on Falls Creek, which enters Hetch Hetchy Reservoir as Wapama Falls. Possible campsites exist all around the lake, though it is heavily used and wood is scarce. Geology buffs will delight in the glacial polish, erratics and striations left by the last glacier that covered this area (about 10,000 years ago). The lake's rainbow-trout population is heavily fished.

Our trail crosses Falls Creek below the lake on a bridge, and hikers can loop back on the trail to Hetch Hetchy via Beehive (see Backpack Trail #6).

Backpack Trail #8   **Smith Meadow**

White Wolf to Smith Meadow and Smith Peak

8½ miles one way; net loss 1460′

E3.

Here's a mostly downhill trail into the northwest part of the quadrangle above Hetch Hetchy Reservoir. If you continue down to the Hetch Hetchy Road (shuttle required) from Smith Meadow, nearly the whole trip is downhill. Even if you return to White Wolf on the trail taken in, the out-and-back journey is only moderate in difficulty due to the small overall change in elevation. Whichever way hikers choose to do this trip, the optional jaunt up 7751-foot Smith Peak from Smith Meadow is highly recommended for its commanding view of the Yosemite north country.

Our trek begins at White Wolf and the first 3 miles are described as the day hike to Harden Lake (Day Hike #6). We continue left on the service road past the point where the Harden Lake trail branches right a few yards before the lake. About ¼ mile farther, this road ends at a Park Service corral, and our route continues as a trail between the northeast side of the fenced meadow and the moraine that dams Harden Lake. (Do *not* take the right-branching horse trail up the moraine to the lake here.) We climb ahead gently for ½ mile in red fir, white fir, and lodgepole and Jeffrey pine before the trail levels off. Wildflowers are abundant and variegated in this open forest during midseason: violets, monkey flowers, groundsel, cow parsnip, mountain aster, yarrow, Mariposa lily, forget-me-not, goldenrod, phacelia, delphinium, lupine and buckwheat all brighten the trailside. We also see many broken-off red-fir trees; more than pines, these trees tend to get weakened by heartrot, due to various fungi invading the wood, and then to get broken off by winter storms, especially when winds are fierce and snow lies heavy on their branches.

After a mile or so of rather level walking, we drop down the north side of a small valley tributary to Cottonwood Creek, and then cross over a low ridge into the upper drainage of Cottonwood Creek itself. One can expect to see black bears on this stretch of trail, as well as airborne wildlife such as flickers, sapsuckers, mountain quail, golden-crowned kinglets and pine siskins. This trail is little-used and a hiker is not likely to see anyone else along the way—all very peaceful.

As we approach Cottonwood Creek we see, besides the previous wildflower colors, columbine, Sierra lily, cranesbill, corn lily and shooting star, along with the shrubs azalea, bitter cherry and whitethorn, and some very old Jeffrey pine trees.

About a mile before Smith Meadow our trail crosses the upper reaches of Cottonwood Creek, which may be dry as early as July after a mild winter. Smith Meadow is one of a series of meadows which were linked by trails in this area when animals were much more used for travel than they are now and Smith grazed his sheep here. This is a pleasant lunch or camp spot, with plenty of firewood. There's also a cold-flowing stream coming into the meadow just beyond the signed junction with the trail to Smith Peak at the north side of the meadow.

(The side trail to Smith Peak switchbacks steeply up from the meadow in a forest of mixed conifers towering over manzanita and whitethorn scrub. After ½ mile of steep ascent, the trail climbs more gradually, and a few hundred feet below the summit of Smith Peak it breaks up into a mass of irregular paths through the underbrush. One has to scramble a bit between unglaciated granite outcrops and chinquapin, huckleberry oak and creambush scrub to the north spur of the peak, but the panorama is ample reward. To the north is the Grand Canyon of the Tuolumne River and the upper end of Hetch Hetchy Reservoir; in the east rise Mts. Hoffmann and Conness; to the south and west are rolling mid-elevation ridges and valleys densely carpeted with pine and fir forest, grading into brown foothills. White-throated swifts whiz around the summit, perhaps getting a "high" from the heights and from the view themselves.)

Back in Smith Meadow, we can pick up the trail going west in order to complete this hike as an all-downhill trip ending on the Hetch Hetchy Road, about 2 miles from the reservoir. The trail becomes increasingly overgrown with whitethorn, depending on how recently this little-used trail has been worked on by trail crews. The best guide to staying on it here may be cut logs that indicate the trail location, because the tree blazes are too old and grown over to be seen anymore.

The trail curves back beside Cottonwood Creek, giving us an opportunity to splash in some of the stream's deep, cool pools before finally heading over a divide toward the slopes above the Tuolumne River. As we continue to descend, the

dominant vegetation has changed from high-elevation lodge-pole pine, Jeffrey pine and red fir to sugar pine, ponderosa pine, white fir, incense-cedar, Douglas-fir and black oak—species more characteristic of lower Sierra elevations.

Beyond a small pond, gradually undergoing ecological succession to forest—but meanwhile full of frogs—the trail switchbacks steeply down through dry forest relieved by the yellow of wallflower, the purple of farewell-to-spring and the white of Queen Anne's lace, bringing us to a junction with a trail south to Mather Ranger Station. We turn north toward Hetch Hetchy, and the appearance of such vegetation as mountain mahogany and canyon oak indicates we are losing elevation fast. Another mile of switchbacks through oak woodlands takes us past our first running water since Cottonwood Creek, and soon after, we come out on the Hetch Hetchy Road above Poopenaut Valley. From here it's a 2-mile walk or hitchhike to the reservoir.

Lateral Trail #1 — Grant Lakes

Ten Lakes Trail to Grant Lake
1½ miles one way; net loss 400'

Grant Lakes, at the headwaters of Yosemite Creek, lie a mile or so off the Ten Lakes Trail—an easy day's walk in from the Tioga Road. The first 5 miles of the trail to Grant Lakes are described in Backpack Trail #1.

From the summit divide (map section G2) above Ten Lakes, the Grant Lakes trail heads south across mixed meadows of lupine, sagebrush, buckwheat and grasses. We soon drop off the ridge into an open forest of lodgepole and western white pine and mountain hemlock. Our trail swings around a stubby ridge, passes through a couple of wet spots and comes out at the western shore of lower Grant Lake, where the campsites are heavily used and wood is scarce.

Yosemite Falls

The upper lake is slightly less used and is reached by an irregular and difficult ducked route that climbs through clumps of Labrador tea and red heather up the north side of the stream between the two lakes, emerging on the northwest shore near the outlet. Due to heavy use, wood is lacking at this lake also. The levelest campsites are on the east and south sides of the lake. Scenery in this glaciated granite basin is superb, as are the views down the valley of Yosemite Creek; so bring a stove and enjoy it. Both Grant Lakes have rainbow trout and receive moderately heavy fishing pressure.

Lateral Trail #2   **Eagle Peak**

Yosemite Creek Trail to Eagle Peak
2 miles one way; net gain 980'

Standing on Eagle Peak (also called Upper Brother) with the whole of Yosemite Valley laid out below is a matchless experience. The trail to Eagle Peak is here described from the Yosemite Creek trail, ½ mile above Yosemite Falls.

This trail goes west from the Yosemite Creek trail (map section E5) (see Day Hike #1) and crosses Eagle Peak creek under a dense cover of lodgepole pine, Jeffrey pine and red fir that shades bracken ferns and fir seedlings. In early summer mosquito clouds accompany the hiker as he climbs steadily upward.

The trail passes through patches of huckleberry oak accented by scarlet gilia, lupine, Mariposa lily and pennyroyal. The path levels past Eagle Peak Meadows, then ascends again, crossing Eagle Peak creek a second time before coming to a junction.

The El Capitan trail goes off to the right (west) and we continue climbing ahead for ½ mile to the summit of Eagle Peak, a fantastic viewpoint. Visible to the artist, poet and lover are Nevada Fall and Half Dome in the east, Cathedral Peak and Mt.

Conness in the northeast, the Merced River and Yosemite Village below, Sentinel Dome, Cathedral Rocks and Cathedral Spires across the valley, and El Capitan along the rim to the west. White-throated swifts zip across the cliffs. Eagle Peak is a very humbling place to stand, and should not be missed by anyone who loves Yosemite.

Lateral Trail #3   Yosemite Creek Alternate

Tioga Road to Yosemite Creek Trail

3 miles one way; net loss 920′

E3.

This trail connects the Lukens Lake trailhead on the Tioga Road with the Yosemite Creek Trail.

From the signed trailhead 3½ miles west of Yosemite Creek, this trail veers right as it leaves the parking area on the *south* side of the road and descends into red fir forest. Soon crossing one small creek, it turns sharply south and drops toward another creek not shown on the topo. The trail crosses this stream too and winds left over a small rise, finally turning right as it drops to the Old Tioga Road near a "U.S. Benchmark."

Our route crosses the road and passes several old green-and-white metal Park Service signs that give some strange mileages. We continue to descend gently under a cover of red fir near a tributary of Yosemite Creek, where we may be amused by the antics of Douglas squirrels along the trail.

Eventually some irregular-sized, angular rocks indicate that we are walking over a glacial moraine for a while, and then we begin a last, steep downhill section that brings us to a signed junction with the Yosemite Creek Trail (Day Hike #1).

Yosemite Creek Pool

Lateral Trail #4   **Ten Lakes Alternate**

Ten Lakes Trail to Lukens Lake Trail

3½ miles one way; net loss 120′; total gain 660′

Here we describe the lateral connecting the Ten Lakes and Lukens Lake trails for possible alternate routes to and from Ten Lakes.

Two miles north of the Tioga Road (map section F3) this lateral goes west from the Ten Lakes trail (Backpack Trail #1). The path is cut through turf under a stand of lodgepole pines that are being succeeded by red firs. We commence climbing gently and soon cross a small stream with pink shooting stars along its banks. After a shaded 1½-mile climb we pass a low summit in pine and fir forest and begin a moderate descent toward the southwest. The bright and cheerful song of the ruby-crowned kinglet tinkles forth from the surrounding forest.

We cross and then parallel an upper branch of the Middle Fork Tuolumne River, which offers the possibility of some quiet camping "away from it all," as this trail is seldom traveled. Finally we arrive at the junction with the Lukens Lake trail (Day Hike #5).

RECOMMENDED READING

Burt, William H. and Richard P. Grossenheider, *A Field Guide to the Mammals,* Third Edition. Houghton Mifflin Co., Boston, 1976.

Gaines, David, *Birds of the Yosemite Sierra.* Mono Lake Committee, Lee Vining, California, 1977.

Gibbens, Robert P. and Harold F. Heady, *The Influence of Modern Man on the Vegetation of Yosemite Valley.* Yosemite Natural History Association, 1964.

Godfrey, Elizabeth H., *Yosemite Indians.* Yosemite Natural History Association, 1977.

Grater, Russel K., *Discovering Sierra Mammals.* Yosemite Natural History Association, 1978.

Hood, Mary and Bill, *Yosemite Wildflowers and Their Stories.* Flying Spur Press, Yosemite, California, 1969.

Jones, William R., *Domes-Cliffs-Waterfalls.* Yosemite Natural History Association, 1976.

Morgensen, Dana C., *Yosemite Wildflower Trails.* Yosemite Natural History Association, 1975.

Munz, Philip A., *California Mountain Wildflowers.* University of California Press, Berkeley, 1963.

Niehaus, Theodore F. and Charles L. Ripper, *A Field Guide to Pacific States Wildflowers.* Houghton Mifflin Co., Boston, 1981.

Paden, Irene D. and Margaret E. Schlichtmann, *The Big Oak Flat Road.* Holmes Book Company, Oakland, 1959.

Peterson, P. Victor and P. Victor Peterson, Jr., *Native Trees of the Sierra Nevada.* University of California Press, Berkeley, 1974.

Robbins, Chandler S., et al., *Birds of North America.* Golden Press, New York, 1966.

Russell, Carl P., *One Hundred Years in Yosemite.* Yosemite Natural History Association, 1968.

Sargent, Shirley, *John Muir in Yosemite*. Second Edition. Flying Spur Press, Yosemite, California, 1971.

Storer, Tracy I. and Robert L. Usinger, *Sierra Nevada Natural History*. University of California Press, Berkeley, 1963.

Thomas, John Hunter and Dennis R. Parnell, *Native Shrubs of the Sierra Nevada*. University of California Press, Berkeley, 1974.

Trexler, Keith A., *The Tioga Road*. Yosemite Natural History Association, 1961

Other Wilderness Press Publications

Schaffer, Jeffrey P., *Yosemite National Park,* Second Edition, 1983.

Schaffer, Jeffrey P. and Thomas Winnett, *High Sierra Hiking Guide to Tuolumne Meadows,* 1977.

Schifrin, Ben, *High Sierra Hiking Guide to Pinecrest,* 1976.

Winnett, Thomas and Bob and Margaret Pierce, *High Sierra Hiking Guide to Yosemite,* 1974.

Winnett, Thomas and Jason Winnett, *Sierra North,* Fourth Edition, 1982.

Index

Trail notes

Trail notes